SHADOWS OF WAR, FACES OF PEACE

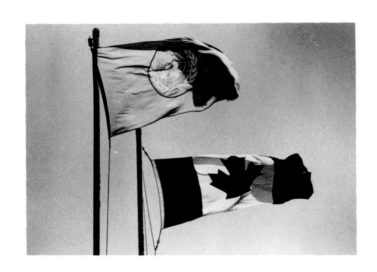

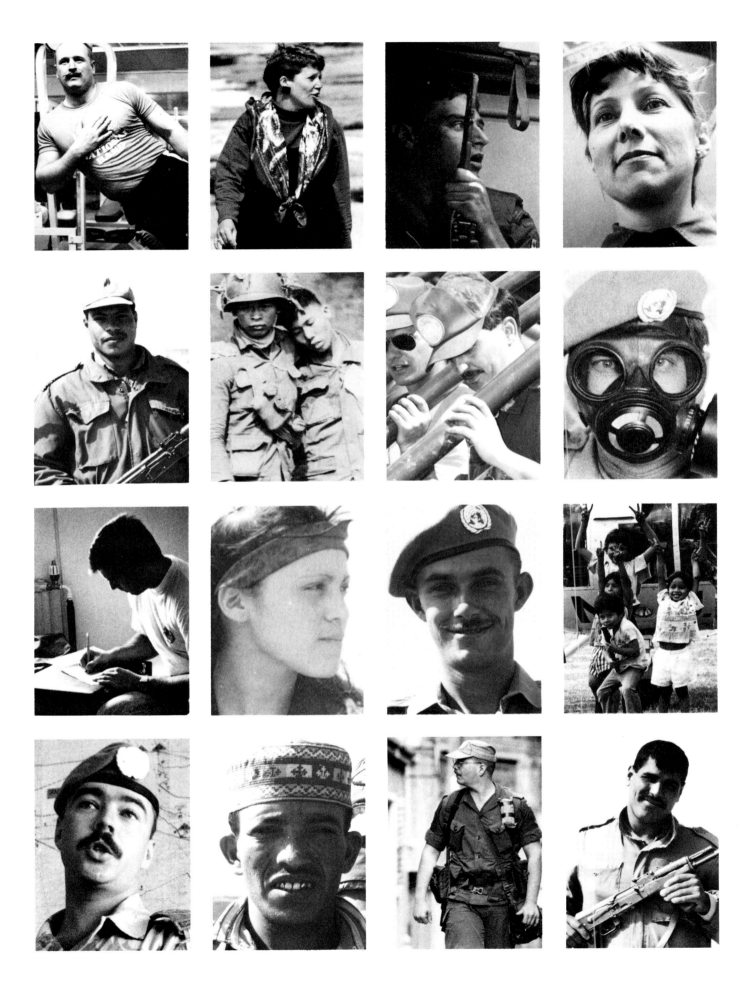

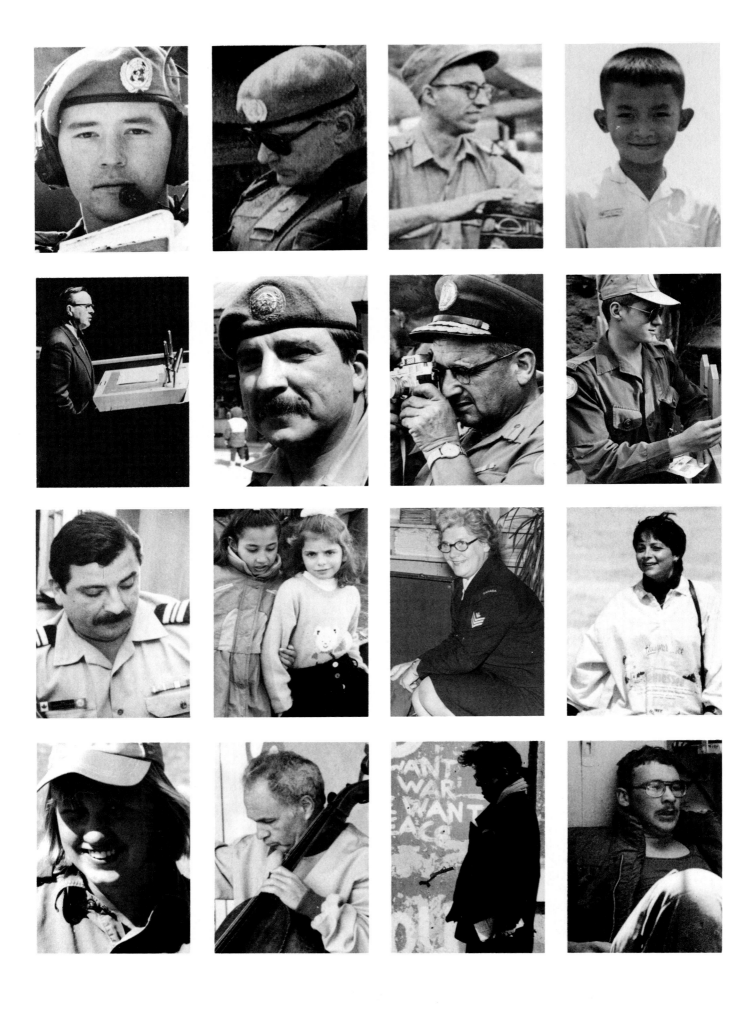

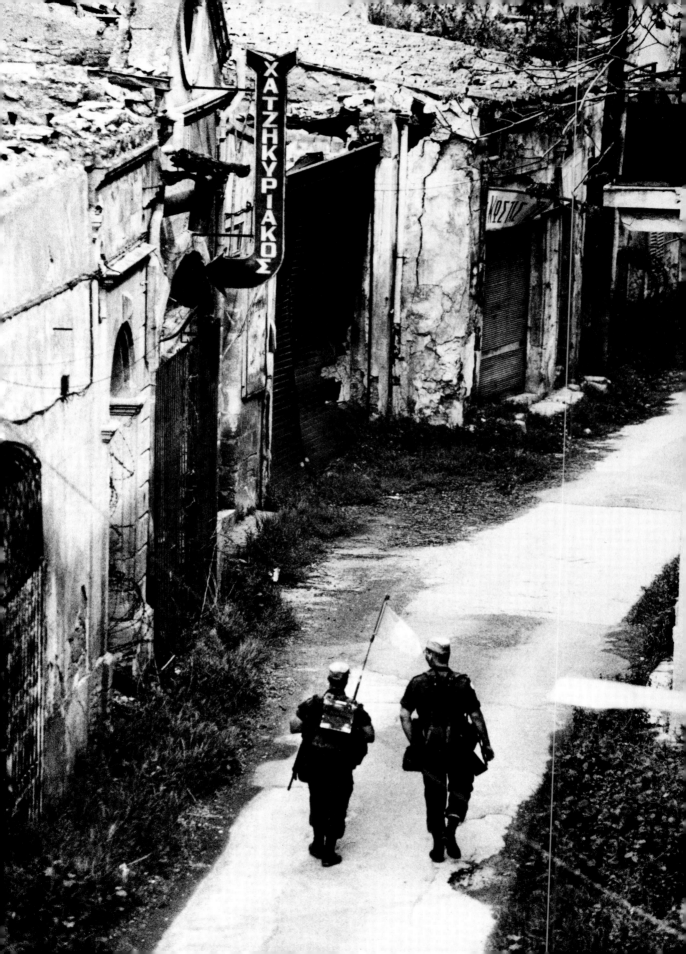

SHADOWS OF WAR, FACES OF PEACE

CANADA'S PEACEKEEPERS

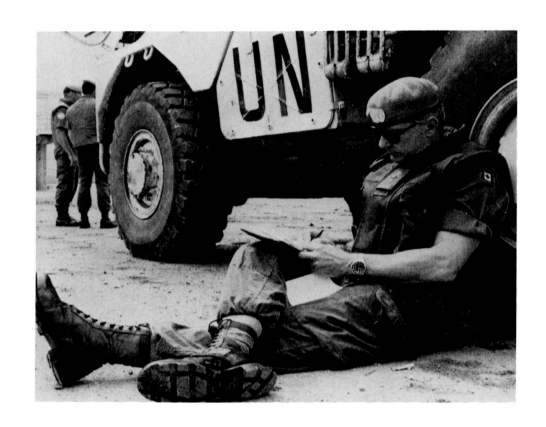

J. L. GRANATSTEIN / DOUGLAS LAVENDER

Photographs by BORIS SPREMO

Based on a film by JOHN MULLER

KEY PORTER BOOKS

Page 1:
Snapping in a fresh breeze, two respected symbols on the Golan Heights fly above Camp Ziouani, home to the Canadian contingent serving with UNDOF.

Page 4:
Patrolling the tense and difficult demilitarized corridor in Nicosia, Pte. François Berube and Pte. Daniel Guevremont (with antenna) walk Nicosia's so-called "green line." Heavily armed Greek and Turkish Cypriot factions are only metres apart here, and routinely taunt one another until a confrontation results.

Previous page:
Maj.-Gen. Lewis MacKenzie, the officer commanding the UN peacekeeping troops in Sarajevo in the summer of 1992, waits on the tarmac as more forces are flown in to secure the city from contending factions.

Contemporary photographs are by Boris Spremo. Other photographs are credited on page 160. Care has been taken to trace ownership of copyright material contained in this book. The publishers will gladly receive any information that will enable them to correct any reference or credit line in subsequent editions.

Canadian Cataloguing in Publication Data
Lavender, Douglas
Shadows of war, faces of peace:
Canada's peacekeepers

ISBN 1-55013-436-1

1. Canada – Armed Forces – Foreign countries – History. 2. United Nations – Armed Forces – History. 3. United Nations – Canada. I. Granatstein, J.L., 1939– . II. Title.

JX1981.P7L38 1992 355'.00971 C92-094705-0

Key Porter Books Limited
70 The Esplanade
Toronto, Ontario
Canada M5E 1R2

Design: Scott Richardson
Typesetting: MacTrix DTP
Maps: Pages

Printed and bound in Canada by
John Deyell Company Limited.

92 93 94 95 96 5 4 3 2 1

CONTENTS

ACKNOWLEDGEMENTS

The Canadian Forces peacekeepers who helped in the compilation of the stories in this book are men and women of informed and infectious optimism. My thanks to Bob Foster, Major Wayne Stuart, and Lieutenant Doug Maybee of the Department of National Defence, Director General Public Affairs, for helping run many of these elusive anecdotes to ground. Thanks also to executive producer Jay Sonley and his assistant, Jacqueline Gélinas, of the Film and Video Centre, Canada Communication Group.

The impetus for the book, and for the television special of the same title, originated with my colleague, film and television producer/director John Muller. His staff at M & M Productions – especially his partner, Henia Muller, production managers Andrea Asbil and Grace Cale, production coordinators Janet Hadjidimitriou and Shar Lenz, and researcher Tracey Dodokin – upheld John's reputation as the "flying Dutchman," turning around volumes of research and transcripts, and handling production details with consistent humour under pressure. The book's French-language version represents the additional contribution of Quebec broadcaster Pierre Nadeau.

Lifting both the personal anecdotes and Jack Granatstein's historical perspectives beyond the written word are the remarkable photographs. These come from three major sources: stills shot on three continents by photojournalist Boris Spremo during production of the television documentary, the personal collections of the peacekeepers, and archival material sourced by photo researcher Lisa Dillon. Gena K. Gorrell provided both captioning and editing expertise.

The following kindly provided products or services: Fuji Photo Film Canada Inc.; Kodak Canada Inc.; Mephisto Canada; Sheraton Tel Aviv Hotel & Towers; Tilley Endurables.

The book is a collaborative effort not unlike, on another scale, the job of peacekeeping itself.

DOUGLAS LAVENDER

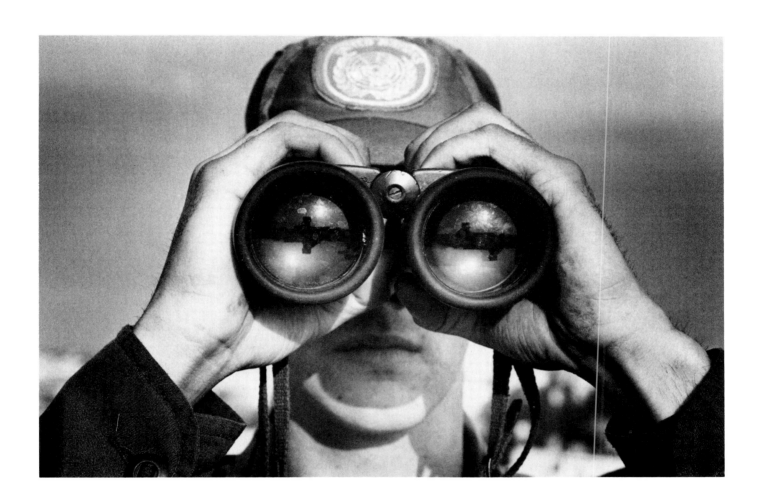

Private Steve Martel of Ancienne Lorette, Quebec, scans the city of Nicosia from his lookout atop Wolseley Barracks.

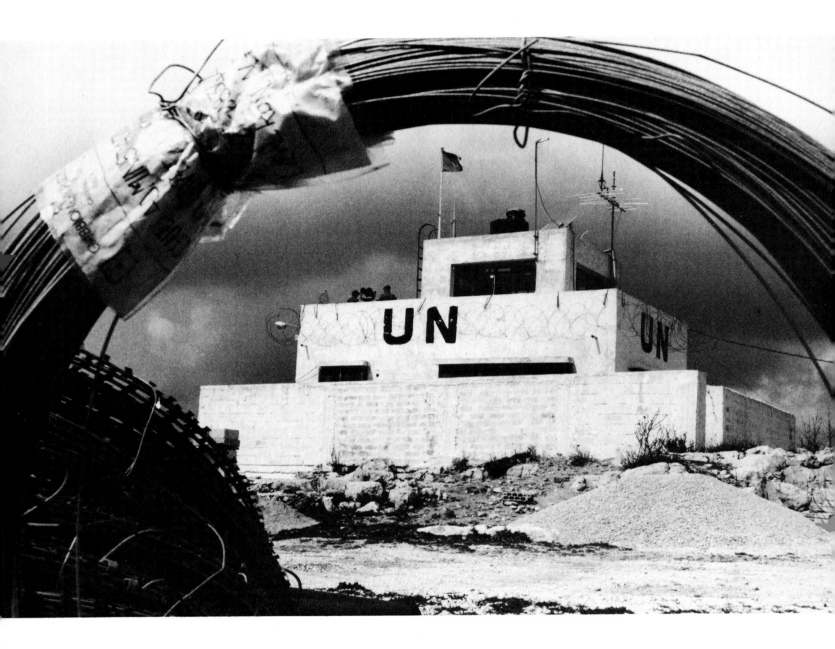

From observation posts
like OP HIN in southern
Lebanon, UN peace-
keepers report armistice
violations on the ground
or in the air.

THE INDISPENSABLE PEACEKEEPER

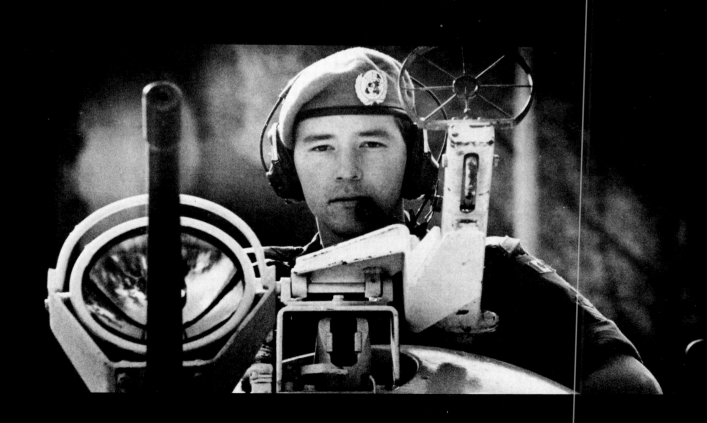

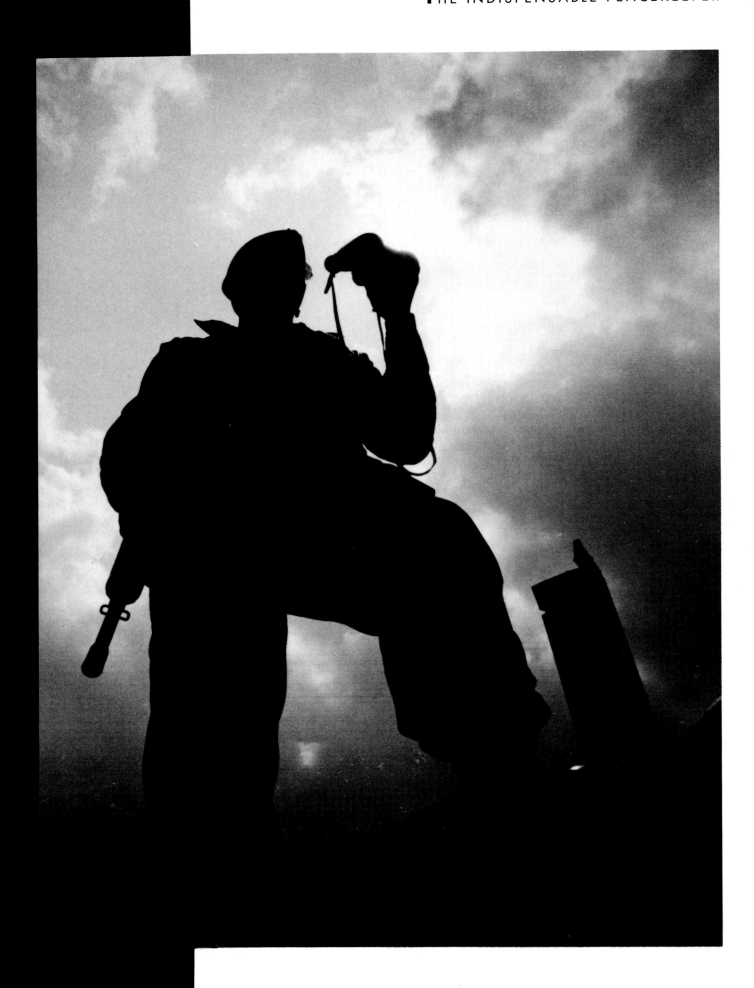

AS THE WORLD MOVED towards war in the Persian Gulf in the last months of 1990, a great debate raged in Canada. Should this country take part in the United Nations–authorized buildup of the coalition against Iraq by sending ships, aircraft, and troops? Should those forces engage in hostilities if it came to war? And if so, what would such participation do to Canada's acceptability for any future request from the United Nations for peacekeepers?

The critics of the government's eventual decision to send men and women from the Canadian Armed Forces to the Gulf and to employ them in the brief, violent assault against the Iraqis were genuinely concerned about the nation's proud record of peacekeeping. Was this now to be squandered by participation in a shooting war?

By the time the war was concluded, before the end of February 1991, the 2,200 Canadian pilots, ground crew, sailors, infantry, and medical personnel had played a small but important part. Canada's servicemen and servicewomen had demonstrated that they were as efficient in a combat zone as they had always been in past wars and in dozens of peacekeeping operations. But that question of their future usefulness in peacekeeping still hung over the country.

Not for long. Within days of the end of the war in the Gulf, the United Nations authorized the establishment of the UN Iraq–Kuwait Observation Mission (UNIKOM), and very quickly Canada was asked to provide army engineers to help lift the thousands of mines the defeated Iraqis had left behind them. Other mine-clearing teams from Britain, France, Pakistan, Egypt, and Bangladesh were also sought, but the Canadians had one of the most dangerous chores, that of clearing the demilitarized zone between Iraq and Kuwait. Clearly, Canada's usefulness in peacekeeping had not been impaired by its service in the Gulf War. The critics, however, were not yet silenced – would we still be acceptable in other parts of the world?

This question too was soon answered. On April 29, 1991, the UN Security Council decided to create MINURSO, the French acronym for the UN Mission for the Referendum in Western Sahara. MINURSO was an attempt to bring to an end a long-lasting war between Morocco and Polisario Front guerrillas seeking the creation of an independent Saharan Arab Democratic Republic. To help in this daunting task in the world's greatest desert, Canada was asked to supply a battalion of infantry, the force commander, RCMP officers, and even some officials from Elections Canada. MINURSO's deployment was to be delayed – the request of Canada was nonetheless significant.

There was soon additional evidence, if any was necessary, that peacekeeping had become *the* favoured approach of the United Nations for the 1990s, and that Canada remained essential to this task. In January 1992, Canada agreed to send

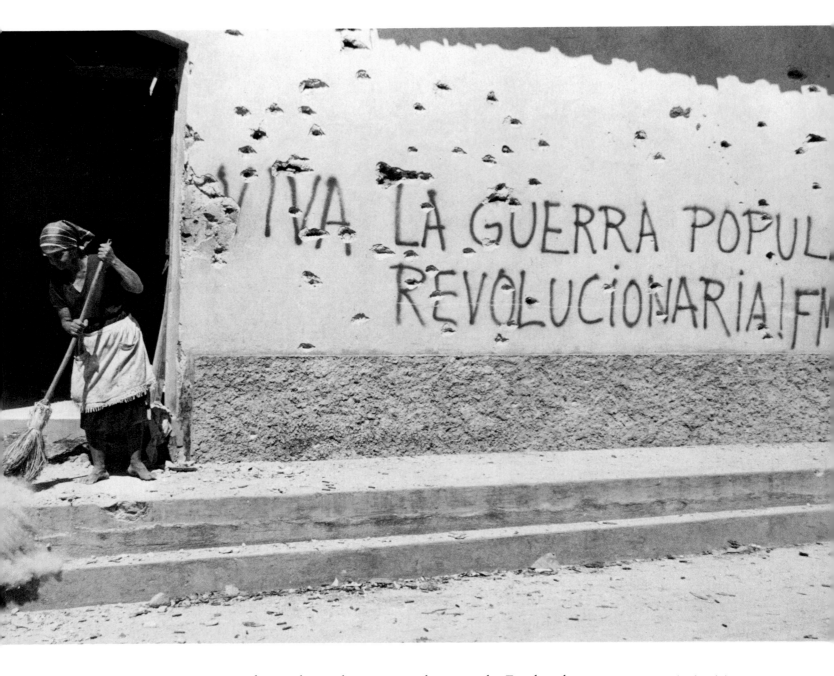

observers to monitor a ceasefire in the twelve-year war between the Farabundo Martí National Liberation Front and the government of El Salvador. For Cambodia, a land devastated by war for more than a generation and still the scene of vicious fighting, the Security Council agreed early in 1992 to establish the UN Transitional Authority in Cambodia (UNTAC), a peacekeeping force designed to run the country, demobilize guerrilla factions, and supervise the return of refugees until elections can be held in 1993. This massive, expensive operation was scheduled to involve 22,000 peacekeepers and to include 200 Canadian specialists. At the same time, a UN delegation of technical experts headed by a retired Canadian military officer was in Somalia, trying to determine if UN peacekeepers could be of use in that East African country ravaged by a prolonged war.

Sweeping aside the debris of endless violence, Salvadorans in Chalatenango, north of San Salvador, opened their doors to the promise of a UN-brokered peace. But healing the wounds that scar every part of the country also marked Salvadorans young and old.

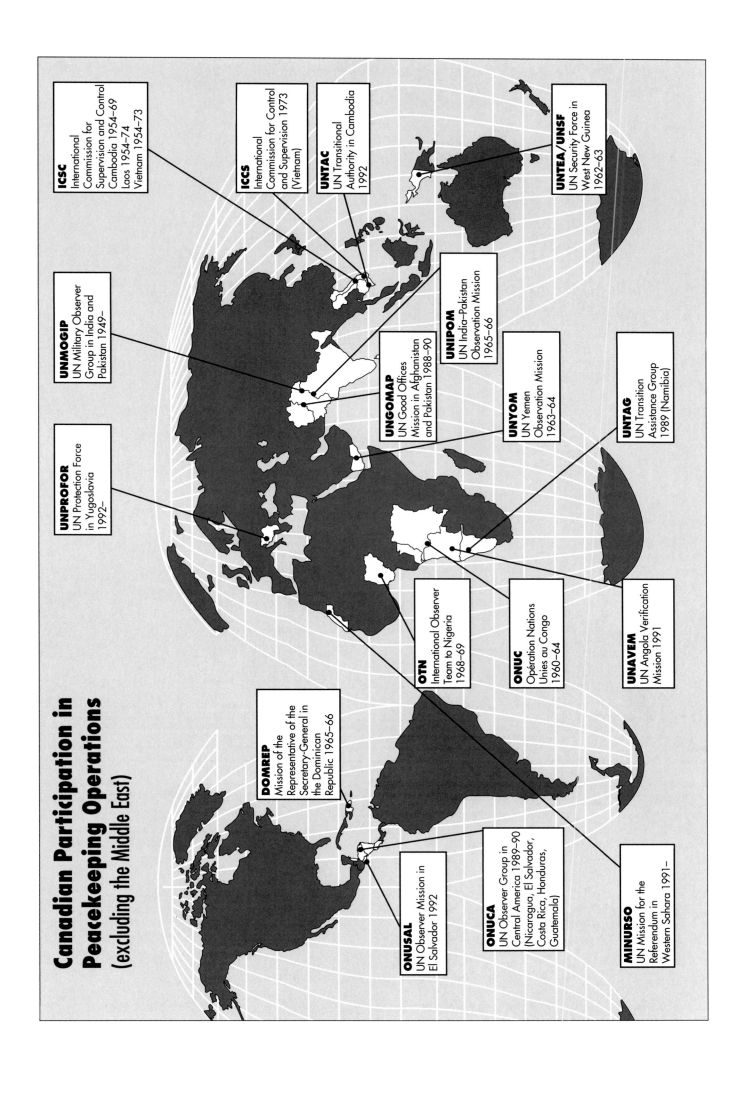

Canadian Participation in Peacekeeping Operations
(excluding the Middle East)

ICSC
International Commission for Supervision and Control
Cambodia 1954–69
Laos 1954–74
Vietnam 1954–73

ICCS
International Commission for Control and Supervision 1973 (Vietnam)

UNTAC
UN Transitional Authority in Cambodia 1992

UNTEA/UNSF
UN Security Force in West New Guinea 1962–63

UNMOGIP
UN Military Observer Group in India and Pakistan 1949–

UNGOMAP
UN Good Offices Mission in Afghanistan and Pakistan 1988–90

UNIPOM
UN India–Pakistan Observation Mission 1965–66

UNYOM
UN Yemen Observation Mission 1963–64

UNTAG
UN Transition Assistance Group 1989 (Namibia)

UNPROFOR
UN Protection Force in Yugoslavia 1992–

OTN
International Observer Team to Nigeria 1968–69

ONUC
Opération Nations Unies au Congo 1960–64

UNAVEM
UN Angola Verification Mission 1991

DOMREP
Mission of the Representative of the Secretary-General in the Dominican Republic 1965–66

ONUSAL
UN Observer Mission in El Salvador 1992

ONUCA
UN Observer Group in Central America 1989–90 (Nicaragua, El Salvador, Costa Rica, Honduras, Guatemala)

MINURSO
UN Mission for the Referendum in Western Sahara 1991–

Then there was Yugoslavia. Two of the constituent republics of that Balkan nation, Slovenia and Croatia, demanded independence and waged a civil war through 1991 to secure it. Bosnia-Herzegovina, yet another Yugoslavian republic, also broke away after a referendum in early 1992. Canada's prime minister, Brian Mulroney, had been among the first world leaders to call for the UN to intervene in the communal fighting, and in March 1992, after many false starts and despite serious continuing outbreaks of hostilities, the UN Protection Force began to move into "protected enclaves", secure zones along the disputed borders. UNPROFOR, as it was called, was expected to number 14,000, and Canada was to contribute the force's chief of staff and some 1,200 infantry and engineers for a six-month stint. The first Canadians arrived in Croatia from their NATO bases at Lahr and Baden-Soellingen, Germany, to begin establishing their headquarters at Daruvar in the fourth week in March.

The evidence was more than conclusive: the need for United Nations initiatives to damp down conflict was more pronounced than ever before – and the ethnic, linguistic, and territorial troubles erupting within the borders of the former Soviet Union suggested that even greater demands were still to come. Those who had feared that Canadians might no longer be welcome as peacekeepers because of their active role in the Gulf War had been wrong; Canadian participation was still a vital element of UN operations.

Canada has a small population and relatively small military forces, yet its troops are called on again and again to don the famous blue berets (and blue helmets) of the United Nations, and to serve under the international peacekeeping flag. Why is this so? What is it about Canada and its armed forces that, for close to a half-century, has made this country's participation so indispensable? With its photographs and text, this book will attempt to answer these questions.

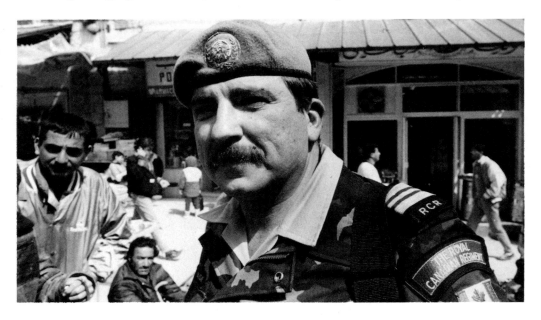

"Jerusalem is a unique city," says Major Haydar, near the Damascus Gate. "Three major world religions hold this city dear. For a peacekeeper this complicates matters. In a sense, it is a universal city. Everybody has some claim to Jerusalem."

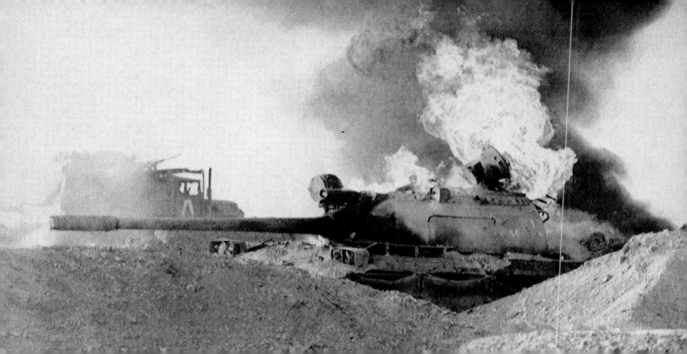

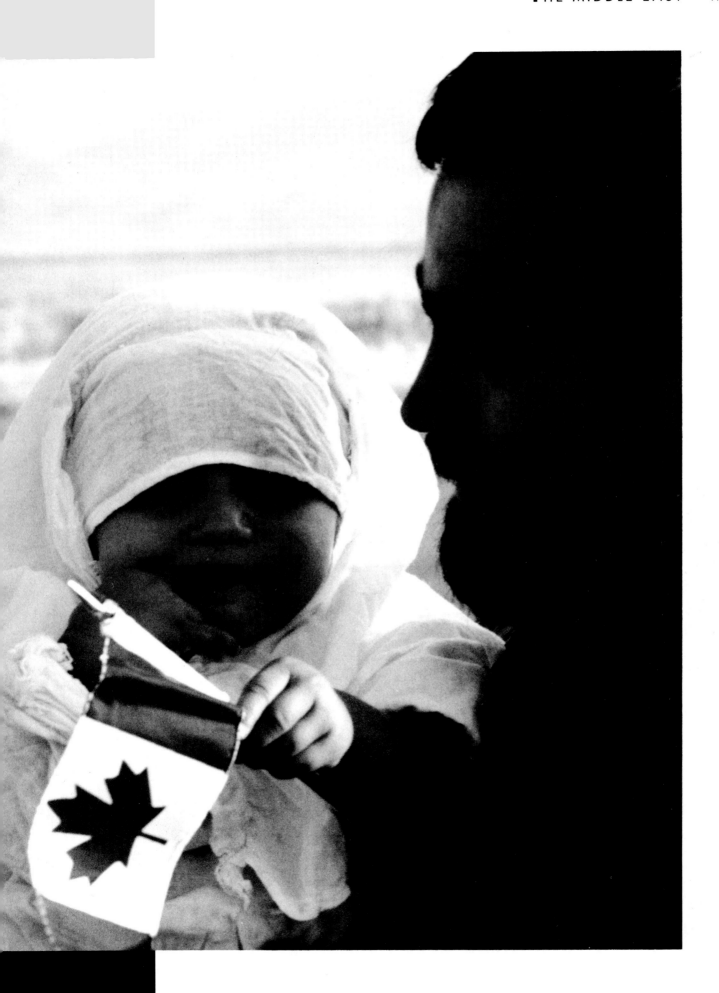

IN THE MONTHS AFTER the end of the Second World War, the world was in a state of continuing chaos. The exhilaration of the victorious Allies was quickly replaced by the onset of the Cold War and the start of a new era of international tension. The United Nations, founded in San Francisco during the spring of 1945, had inspired great hopes around the globe, but the optimism had been dashed by the revelations of East–West hostility that quickly embroiled its General Assembly and Security Council.

One victim was the elaborate scheme for collective security that the drafters of the UN Charter had been planning. The founders had envisaged large international armed forces equipped with great naval and air fleets to impose the world body's will on aggressor states. Political infighting at UN headquarters in New York left those plans mere paper; all the first Secretary-General could muster by 1949 was a UN Field Service of 300 men that was designed to perform technical tasks.

The United Nations therefore had nothing in hand to deal with the crisis that erupted in the Middle East in 1947. Great Britain, weakened by the human and financial losses of the war, had announced that it was surrendering its mandate over Palestine. Arab and Jewish residents, who had both resented the British presence, fell into bitter communal fighting. On May 14, 1948, the Jewish area of Palestine proclaimed its independence as the State of Israel and fended off the armies of Egypt, Lebanon, Jordan, and Syria, as well as the attacks of Palestinians. In August 1948 a more-or-less firm truce was finally put in place under the UN's aegis, and eventually Israel and its angry neighbours signed armistices that were to be overseen by the first UN peacekeeping operation, the United Nations Truce Supervision Organization (UNTSO).

UNTSO's officer observers were few in number and overworked in their efforts to cope with the flood of complaints from both sides of the armistice lines.

PAGE 18:

Flames and acrid smoke rage and billow from a trench-bound Iraqi tank. Behind it, the Allied advance pushes steadily across Kuwait during the final stages of the 1991 Gulf War.

PREVIOUS PAGE:

Flying a welcome flag, an Iranian revolutionary guardsman and his daughter greet Canadians at the Bakhtaran airport.

The border between Israel and Jordan. The Second World War was barely over when Israel proclaimed its independence and the Middle East became the scene of new hostilities. By June 1948 the fledgeling UN had its Truce Supervision Organization in place.

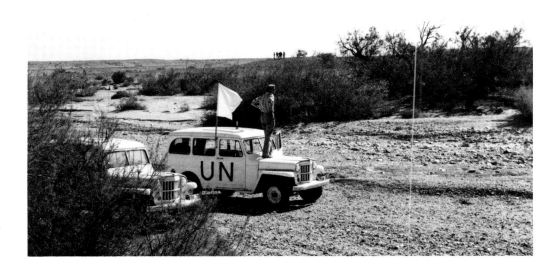

Tensions remained high in the region as Arab guerrilla attacks inevitably provoked heavy Israeli air and ground responses, setting off chain reactions of strikes and counterstrikes. In 1953, UNTSO was increased in strength, and for the first time the Secretary-General asked Canada to contribute officer observers. The army provided four officers in February 1954, and later that same year Major-General E.L.M. Burns, a wartime corps commander in Italy and the post-war Deputy Minister of Veterans Affairs, became UNTSO's chief of staff. Burns's task was an unenviable one, as this dour man (whose wartime nickname was "Smiler" because he never did) was obliged to try to keep the peace between antagonists with generations of hatred and mistrust between them. His observers, posted into this cauldron for a year's tour of duty, suffered as well, their efforts viewed with suspicion by Arabs and Israelis alike, and their persons occasionally coming under fire or falling victim to mines. UNTSO continues its hazardous, thankless task to this day.

General Burns's moment came on October 29, 1956, when Israel launched a devastating attack against President Nasser's Egypt. The world was thrown into turmoil. For a week the Israeli tanks advanced, occupying Egypt's Sinai Desert, and the British and French – who were, in fact, secretly in league with Israel – issued ultimatums against the warring parties. When Britain and France launched their own attack against Egypt, world war seemed an imminent possibility. The way out was provided by Lester Pearson, Canada's Secretary of State for External Affairs. Deeply grieved by the actions of Canada's two mother countries, and troubled by the hostility that had reached gale force between Washington and London, Pearson produced the germ of an idea at the UN on the night of November 1. "I regret the use of military force," he told the General Assembly, adding that what was needed was "consideration of the best way to bring about that kind of cease-fire which would have enduring and beneficial results." And what was that? Pearson had the answer: "a United Nations force large enough to keep these borders at peace while a political settlement is being worked out. . . . My own Government would be glad to recommend Canadian participation in such a United Nations force, a truly international peace and police force." That idea – a force drawn from the armies of member nations, for the specific needs of the crisis – was the genesis of the United Nations Emergency Force (UNEF), which General Burns would command. It won Pearson the Nobel Peace Prize.

UNEF was hastily improvised in New York and in the Middle East. Burns created a tiny staff from UNTSO while Pearson, the Secretary-General, and a few others cobbled together an international army from the offers that came in. Almost at once the Egyptians raised objections. They had been attacked, they

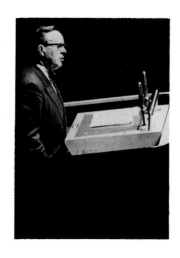

"Peace," proclaimed Lester B. Pearson, addressing the UN General Assembly during the Suez Crisis, "is far more than ceasing to fire."

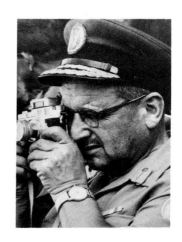

Gen. E.L.M. Burns, commander of UNEF I forces. The exasperated Burns noted that in the Middle East "no matter how hard one tried to be objective and impartial, if one accepted the views of one side on any matter, the other side accused one of partiality."

The first Canadians arrive in Egypt for UNEF I, in November 1956. By January 1957 over 1,000 Canadians were involved, but because Egypt identified Canada with the British aggressors, they did mainly administrative and technical work.

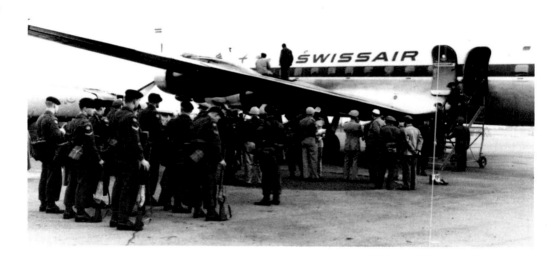

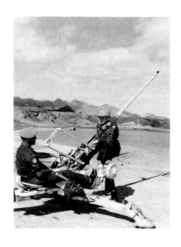

Canadian soldiers check out an Egyptian anti-aircraft gun in the Sinai peninsula in 1958.

protested, and now the UN was sending troops into the Sinai. Under the circumstances, they insisted on having some say in the composition of UNEF. This seemed reasonable. But to Ottawa's chagrin, the Egyptians objected to Canada being part of UNEF – despite Pearson's contribution. Egypt was adamant: Britain was one of the aggressors, and Canadian troops wore British-pattern uniforms; their flag, the Red Ensign, had a Union Jack in the corner; even the name of the infantry regiment selected for UNEF duty, the Queen's Own Rifles, reeked of Empire. Ruefully the Queen's Own, who had already reached Halifax, headed back to their Calgary barracks. Instead, Nasser agreed that Canada should provide administrative units, those unglamorous but essential troops without which the force could not operate. In 1956, without Egyptian objection, Burns asked for a Canadian air force communications squadron and logistical and signals units, as well as an armoured reconnaissance squadron. By January 1957, Canada had 1,100 troops in Egypt, one-sixth of UNEF's strength.

Why, in the face of Cairo's objections, was Canada allowed to contribute at all? The reason was simple necessity. The Great Powers – Britain, France, the United States, China, and Russia – had been barred from any contributions to UNEF, and very few potential contributor nations had armed forces with sophisticated logistics and communications capacity. Because of its tradition of sending troops abroad in wartime, and because of its contributions to the North Atlantic Treaty Organization (NATO), Canada did. In the crisis of 1956, even the suspicious Egyptians had to recognize that.

UNEF was a new venture for the United Nations. It was much larger than earlier observer forces but it was not a combatant army. It had no ships, no fighter aircraft, no tanks – only lightly armed infantry, air transport, and a handful of armoured cars. Its work, after the excitement of the first few months and after Israel had withdrawn from the Sinai, was prosaic in the extreme, and the

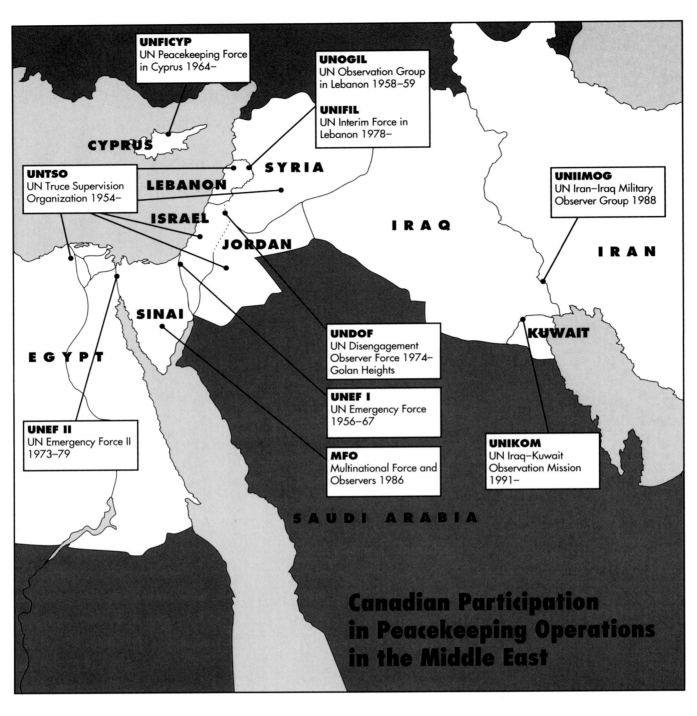

UNFICYP
UN Peacekeeping Force
in Cyprus 1964–

UNOGIL
UN Observation Group
in Lebanon 1958–59

UNIFIL
UN Interim Force in
Lebanon 1978–

UNTSO
UN Truce Supervision
Organization 1954–

UNIIMOG
UN Iran–Iraq Military
Observer Group 1988

CYPRUS

SYRIA

LEBANON

ISRAEL

JORDAN

IRAQ

IRAN

SINAI

UNDOF
UN Disengagement
Observer Force 1974–
Golan Heights

KUWAIT

EGYPT

UNEF I
UN Emergency Force
1956–67

UNEF II
UN Emergency Force II
1973–79

MFO
Multinational Force and
Observers 1986

UNIKOM
UN Iraq–Kuwait
Observation Mission
1991–

SAUDI ARABIA

Canadian Participation in Peacekeeping Operations in the Middle East

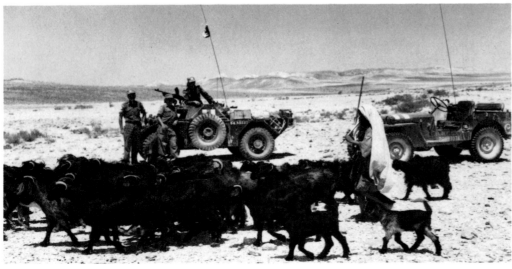

A desert patrol of a
Canadian reconnaissance
squadron in the first
UNEF operation pauses
in the Sinai in 1957
to watch a goatherd
serenade his goats.

Charred skeleton of an Egyptian train bombed by Israel during the Six Day War. The war left Israel occupying territory from the Suez Canal to the Golan Heights and the Jordan River, but 25 years later the scars – and the enmity – remain.

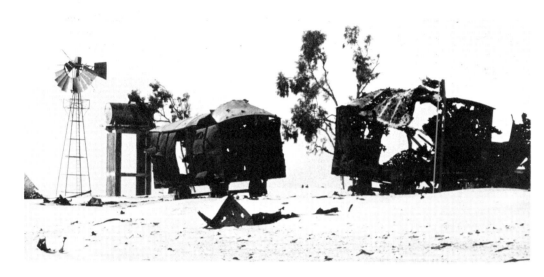

Two Canadians with UNDOF inspect the crumbling ruins of Kuneitra, a Syrian town. More than 54 Arab settlements were abandoned when an estimated 70,000 Syrians fled the 1967 Israeli advance on the Golan Heights.

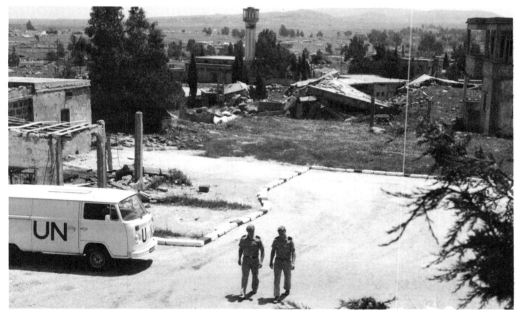

Canadian troops performed tasks very much like those they had in Canada or with NATO. Still, there was a chance for leave in exotic locales such as Cairo, Jerusalem, Beirut, or Cyprus, and there was the belief, the genuine belief, that they were helping to maintain peace in one of the critical areas of the world. That sense ended dramatically in 1967.

Trouble along the Syrian–Israeli border had been endemic for years, but in early 1967 it escalated sharply. There were threats and counter-threats from Damascus and Jerusalem, and Nasser, the self-proclaimed leader of the Arab world, sent his army back into the Sinai on May 15. Two days later, the Egyptian president demanded that the UN withdraw UNEF from its positions along the Israeli–Egyptian border; the Secretary-General agreed. The next day, Nasser demanded that UNEF withdraw from Egypt altogether. New York accepted this as well, and the rush to war was on. Lester Pearson, by now prime minister, tried

to intervene and was called an "idiot" for his pains by Nasser, and the Egyptian leader ordered the Canadian forces out of Egypt within forty-eight hours. The air force unit left so hastily that the Canadian flag, forgotten on its flagpole, still waved over the empty base. By May 30, only a rearguard was left.

For all its indignity, this hurried departure spared Canadian troops the casualties that other UNEF troops suffered in the Six Day War, which began on June 5. The fighting left Israel in a commanding military position in the region, once more in possession of the Sinai and with newly conquered territories on Syria's Golan Heights and on the west bank of the Jordan River.

The Israeli victory did nothing to bring peace to the region. Six years later, Egypt struck across the Suez Canal during the Jewish High Holidays while Syria attacked from the north. After heavy fighting and serious losses, Israel withstood the assaults, and in the aftermath two new UN forces took the field. A large force dubbed UNEF II, positioned between Israel and Egypt, involved more than 1,100 Canadians. On the Golan Heights, the United Nations Disengagement Observer Force watched over the Syrian lands still held by the Israelis; more than 200 Canadians served in the logistical unit that maintained UNDOF's vehicles and electronic equipment and provided supply, communications, and medical services.

But the exhaustion of war had at last begun to affect the main protagonists. President Anwar Sadat of Egypt, his country's pride restored by the creditable showing of its forces in the 1973 war, broke the circle of violence and suspicion and offered to make peace with Israel, and American president Jimmy Carter ultimately brokered a settlement. To watch the Sinai, evacuated by Israel and returned to Egypt, a new peacekeeping force, the Multinational Force and Observers, was put in place. The MFO did not involve the United Nations, because the Soviet

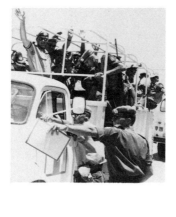

In May of 1967 Canada opposed Egypt's domination of the Gulf of Aqaba, Israel's only access to the Red Sea; Nasser called Pearson an "idiot" and ordered Canadian troops out within 48 hours. The hasty departure was embarrassing, but saved Canadian lives; a week later Israel launched the Six Day War.

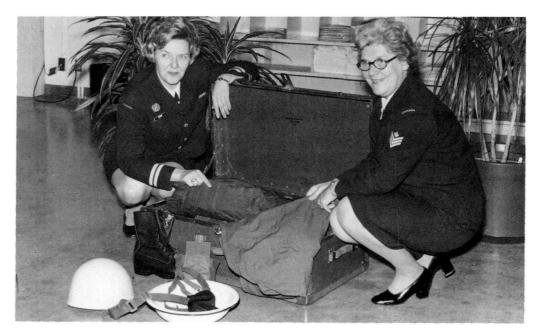

In 1973 Canadians returned to Egypt, as part of UNEF II. Here, the first two women soldiers to join the force pack their kit boxes in 1975. Heat and disease were major difficulties for Canadian forces, but many felt the boredom was even worse.

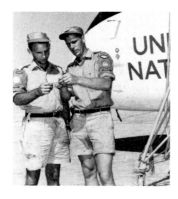

A de Havilland Caribou
gets an overhaul from
UNEF I airmen in El
Arish, Egypt, in 1963.
Despite its large payload,
the Caribou could take
off in a tight 220 metres.

Union, which had sided with Syria, would not back such a mission. It did, however, soon require Canadian helicopters and 140 Canadian service personnel.

Israel and its Arab enemies constituted the main flashpoint in the region, but not the only one. In 1958, Lebanon, until then a relatively tranquil, prosperous country where Christians and Muslims shared power, began a long slide into factionalism. As Arab nations jostled for influence there, the United Nations dispatched UNOGIL, the UN Observation Group in Lebanon, to watch the borders. Seventy-seven unarmed Canadians participated in the force, which disbanded in 1959, peace once more restored.

But the problems there were far from solved. Palestinian guerrilla factions began to use Lebanon as a base to launch raids against Israel, each one of which provoked massive retaliation and large armed incursions. To confirm the withdrawal of Israeli forces from Lebanon in 1978, the UN sent in another large peacekeeping force, optimistically named the United Nations Interim Force in Lebanon; 117 Canadians took part. But despite its peak 7,000-person strength, UNIFIL could do little to control the Palestinian attacks or the Israeli retaliations. In 1982, Israeli Prime Minister Menachem Begin sent his country's army into Lebanon in force to crush Palestinian bases and refugee camps. The costly, bloody war ultimately resulted in the temporary expulsion of the Palestinians and the *de facto* control of most of Lebanon by Syria, while Israel exercised occupation of the south through a surrogate Christian-Arab militia. The Palestinians soon returned, the guerrilla raids resumed, and civil war broke out. Lebanon – the long-time pearl of the Middle East – was occupied, divided, destroyed. It became a monument to the costs of war. UNIFIL remained but was effectively paralysed, its members in constant peril.

In Yemen, meanwhile – a country of vast deserts at the bottom of the Arabian peninsula – a rebellion against the feudal monarch in 1962 had led to internal

A de Havilland Otter is a
welcome visitor in El
Arish, Egypt, during
UNEF I operations.
The versatile bushplane
proved as valuable in
deserts and tropical
jungles as it was in
Canada's northlands.

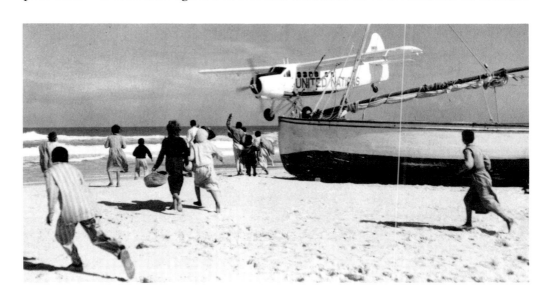

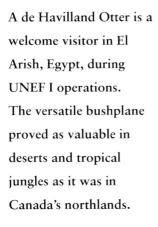

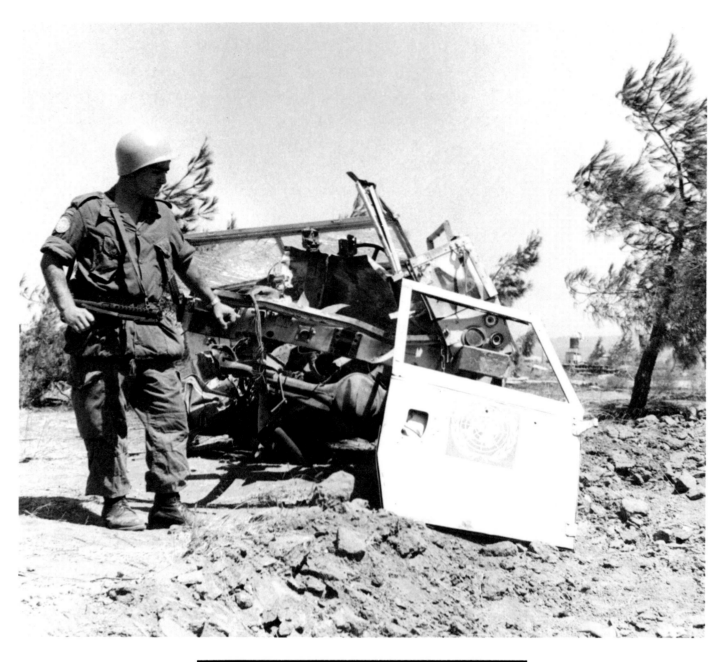

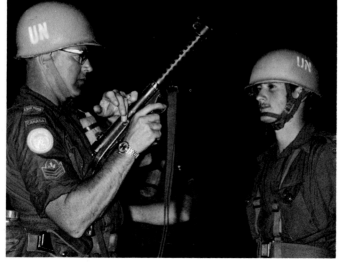

ABOVE:
Too often the peacekeepers become victims. Here, a Canadian corporal looks over the jeep in which four Austrian UNEF II soldiers died in 1974. Not far away, nine Canadians were killed when their de Havilland Buffalo was shot down.

Canadian peacekeepers check and recheck their weapons before heading out on duty for UNIFIL, the armed "interim" UN operation that began in Lebanon in 1978.

fighting, while neighbouring states and Great Powers hovered anxiously. In June 1963, the Security Council voted to create the UN Yemen Observation Mission, a small force employing air and ground patrols. Canada was asked, and duly agreed, to provide fixed-wing aircraft and helicopters and thirty-six officers and men. Although the fighting continued into 1967, the UN withdrew the force in September 1964, after the Secretary-General concluded that the threat to peace and security had diminished.

More serious, because the countries involved were more populous and because vast oil reserves were at stake, was the war between Iran and Iraq that began in 1980. The Western-oriented Iraqis, led by Saddam Hussein's military government, invaded strategic southern regions of Muslim fundamentalist Iran, a country that had deposed the shah and turned viciously against the Americans and westerners who had propped up the Pahlevi dynasty. The war raged for eight years, until both attacker and defender were exhausted and the UN finally felt able to intervene. The UN Iran–Iraq Military Observer Group, authorized in August 1988, took the field to separate the combatants, supervise the ceasefire, and help speed the exchange of prisoners. Canada provided UNIIMOG's signals squadron and a number of observers, in all 510 officers and men, based in Tehran and Baghdad. In the light of subsequent events in the Gulf, it is ironic that Canadians found the Iraqis far easier to deal with than the Iranians. For the troops the worst difficulties arose from obsolete radio equipment, all that the cash-strapped Canadian Armed Forces had, and the heat. Still, the task was accomplished. The

Inadvertent roommates, a Canadian corporal and a small lizard hold differing views on eviction rights; the corporal discovered the creature taking up residence in her quarters.

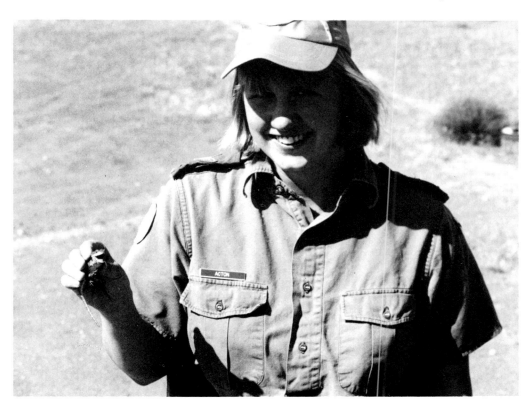

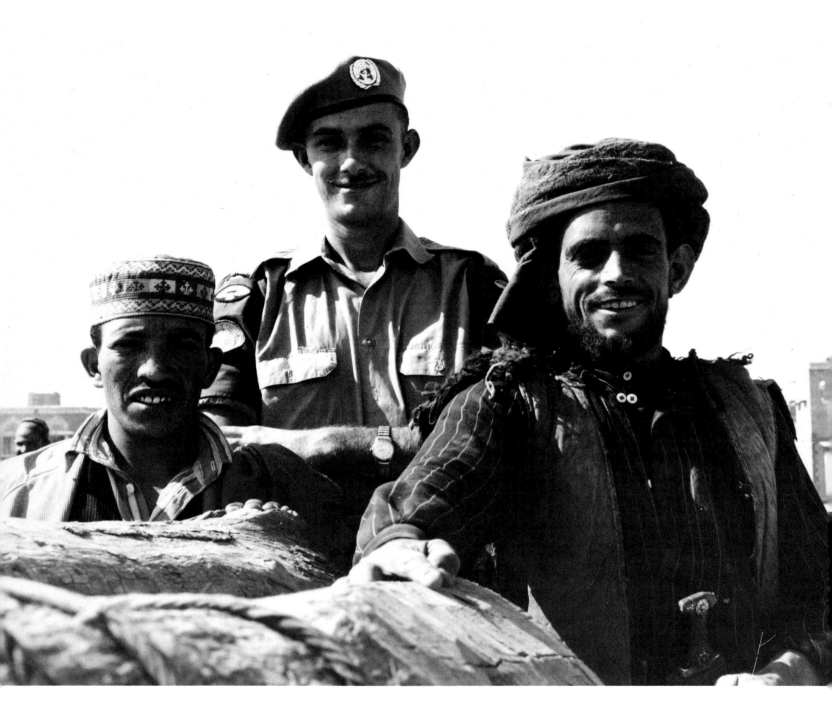

Peacekeeping sites are
often dangerous, but
they can also be exotic.
This soldier from Nova
Scotia made new acquain-
tances in Sana, the capital
of Yemen.

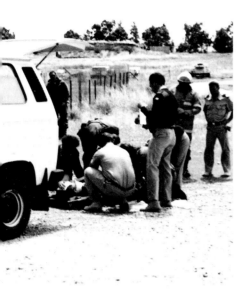

An emergency on the Golan draws a priority response from a Canadian Canlog UNDOF medical team. The casualty will be air-med evacuated to Ram Bam Hospital in Haifa, Israel.

A camel train passes Canadians in the RCAF serving with UNYOM. In the background is Sana, the walled capital city.

signallers returned to Canada before Christmas 1988, though 15 observers stayed on watch until 1990.

But Saddam Hussein's regime was not yet ready to abandon military adventurism. In August 1990, the Iraqis invaded and conquered a tiny neighbour, Kuwait. After negotiations and economic sanctions produced no results, the United Nations, pushed and prodded by the United States, mounted a vast coalition effort and destroyed much of Saddam's military force – and country – in a brutal but quick war that ended in an Iraqi surrender in February 1991. To watch over the borderlands, the UN put yet another force, the UN Iraq–Kuwait Observation Mission (UNIKOM), on the ground. More than 300 Canadian military engineers took part, removing and destroying the vast arsenal of abandoned weaponry, unexploded bombs, and thousands of boobytraps and mines left behind by the Iraqis. This dangerous task was handled with consummate skill.

The number of peacekeeping forces created in the Middle East – ten in all, over less than forty-five years – stands as stark testimony to the unresolved tensions in a large, critical region. Keeping the peace is obviously necessary, but unless there is a will to make peace, the endless cycle of violence goes on. Because that will is absent among so many of the combatants, the UN's efforts at piling observer force atop disengagement team have largely failed. Still, that has not been Canada's fault. From Lester Pearson's role in creating UNEF through to the nation's participation in every one of the forces deployed in the region, Canada has done its part.

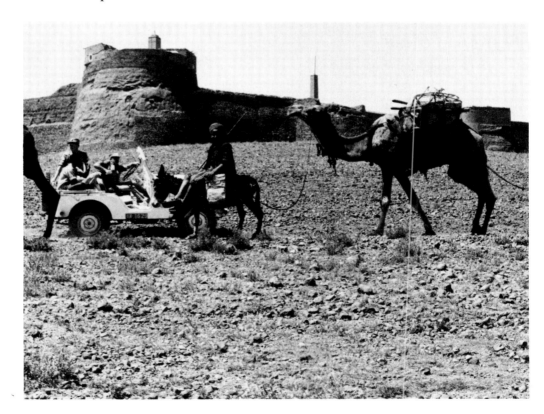

A BLOODY GOOD SOLDIER

Major Gilbert Côté

Lebanon

For me, the big thing about serving as a UN military observer in Lebanon was that it approached what I felt were the conditions we would face in combat. Day in and day out we were confronting threats, coming under fire. An operation like that forces you to face the kind of fears a soldier has to control.

On my second tour, in 1987, I took charge of Team X-Ray. An Irish officer was assigned to my team, but he wasn't able to start right away. So I went down to headquarters and asked a young Australian captain, Peter McCarthy, if he would replace the other man temporarily.

We loaded Peter's gear into my jeep, and I offered to show him the gullies that different factions used to infiltrate the area.

On the way, we came to a blind curve in the road. I heard this great noise from an oncoming vehicle just up around the bend. It was an armoured personnel carrier, although we couldn't see it at that point. I knew they wouldn't be able to stop, so I steered for the ditch. It was a very narrow road bordered by trees. We were extremely lucky. The big APC missed us by no more than a few centimetres. We would have been crushed beneath it.

They pulled us out of the ditch and I took a picture of the gang. Then we continued on patrol. That was the last picture ever taken of Peter.

Around noon we started up a serpentine trail leading to a high point from which you could observe about forty kilometres all around. Turning back, we drove onto another trail that crisscrossed ours. The next thing I knew, I was flying through the air.

We had run over a mine. When I found the remnants of the jeep, I found Peter too. I felt for a pulse, but there was nothing.

I woke up in hospital three days later. The guys who

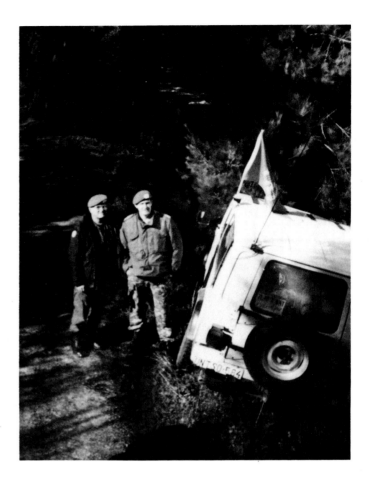

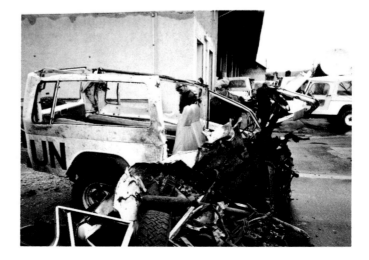

Major Côté (*on right*) and Captain McCarthy pause for a cheerful snapshot of their jeep after a near miss with an oncoming APC. Then the two continued their patrol – and hit a mine. The force of the explosion demolished the jeep and blew the engine right out of it. "I had cracked ribs, a skull fracture, lacerations everywhere," says Major Côté. "But I was alive. Poor Peter wasn't."

had picked me up thought I was a goner. Not only had I gone through a metal roof, but I had walked almost two kilometres in that condition. I had cracked ribs, a skull fracture, lacerations everywhere, fractured hands, a punctured lung, and I was paralyzed on one side. But I was alive. Poor Peter wasn't. It's a crying shame. He was a young up-and-comer in the Australian officer corps, a bloody good soldier. I still feel responsible.

I had to relearn almost everything. I couldn't read. I couldn't write even a simple sentence. To this day I have trouble speaking. But the mind has tremendous poten-

tial. No matter what the experts may tell you, the mind can heal itself, find new circuits.

I've given it a lot of thought. Despite the terrible risks, the work we do with the UN is very, very worthwhile. It serves an extremely important role, keeping the forest fires of war under control.

After his recovery, Major Côté served on the Peacekeeping Desk at National Defence Headquarters until his release in 1991.

SANDWICHES AND SHRAPNEL

SHIRLEY ELMS, KATIE BENNETT

Lebanon

SHIRLEY ELMS:

Beirut in 1983 was the most exciting time in my life. My husband, Captain Geordie Elms, was part of the Canadian contingent assigned peacekeeping duties with the UN Truce Supervision Organization. It was an operation where officers were responsible for their own accommodations, so wives could join them if they wished.

We stayed in a thirteen-storey apartment building. In better days it had been a holiday home, and it was quite nice. We had fresh running water – a lot of the other buildings had salt water. Of course, we also had open drains, and we did have a rat living with us until we terminated that relationship. But all in all, it was a great place to be.

We had a lot of fun. The Canadian wives would shop for groceries together, play cards. Speaking for myself, I'd say we were pretty innocent. I really had no sense of danger. For some reason I thought that, living under the UN flag, we were safe. The war had nothing to do with us; we were just staying with our husbands.

By January, things began to get a little more tense. There were kidnappings on the streets around our

building. There were shootings right outside. It was obviously time to go.

We left Beirut early in the first week of February. We got out just in time; it was the last aircraft out. Katie Bennett was the only Canadian wife left behind.

KATIE BENNETT:

On February 6, after the other Canadian wives had left Beirut, my husband, Captain Gordon Bennett, and I were in our apartment, which happened to overlook a Lebanese army camp. We heard a noise at the door. Young fellows with guns and ammunition were outside. They told us that they were taking over the building, that if we didn't let them in they'd kick the door down.

I looked at these young boy soldiers and thought, "My son is older than that." I figured maybe they were hungry or something, but they went straight to the windows, broke the glass, and started firing at the Lebanese below.

One of these kids lived right next door to us. I knew his mother. I said to him, "Your mother must be terribly worried about you." He most likely thought I was an

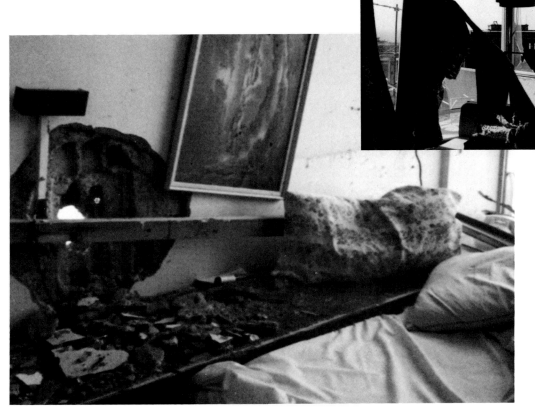

The bedroom of Captain Gordon Bennett and his wife, Katie, after Lebanese militiamen left their Beirut apartment a bullet-torn shambles. "When you get home and stop and think about it," says Katie, "that's when the chills go up your spine."

absolute nut. There I was, crouched on the floor, giving them sandwiches and pop, and asking about their parents.

I felt so sorry for them. That's the way they were brought up. They thought of themselves as underground fighters, defending their home. I'm sure they'd had guns in their hands since birth.

Of course, once they started shooting out, our apartment became a target for the Lebanese. It was getting blown to pieces. My husband and I headed for the basement, but couldn't even make it that far. We were stuck in the stairwell, couldn't get up or down because of the flying bullets. Shells were lying all over the stairway.

We were there for a long, long time before we made it to the basement. We spent a day and a night down there, sitting on the dirt floor while the building above us was being shot to bits. There was a big steel door, and you never knew when it was going to open and whether

you were about to be killed.

About midway through the battle, the funniest thing happened. I suppose somebody had called a ceasefire, because a man came down selling pita bread. Then, after a fifteen-minute lull, it all started up again.

After the fighting finally ended we went back upstairs. The apartment was a shambles, just a shambles. Shrapnel everywhere.

At the time when something like that is happening, it's not as scary as it sounds. But when you get home and stop and think about it, that's when the chills go up your spine. Still, I'd love to go back. February 6 was my birthday.

Katie Bennett was airlifted to safety in Cyprus, where she was later joined by Shirley Elms.

CHRISTMAS IN BEIRUT

MAJOR PHILIP COOK

Lebanon

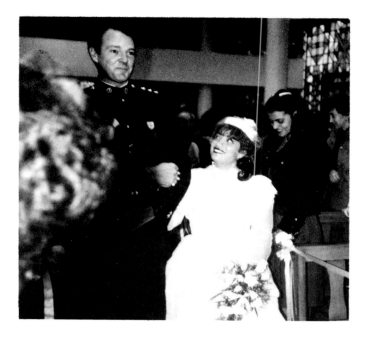

It sounded simple enough. After a briefing at UN Truce Supervision Organization headquarters in Jerusalem, I was to assume observer duty in Beirut. But how exactly was I to get there? This was 1983. Internal conflict in Lebanon was at a high. The Beirut airport was closed, no UN helicopters were flying into the area, and the road from Damascus through the Bekka Valley and onward to Beirut was closed.

This caused some discussion amongst the training team. Finally I was told that I could get a ride with a French logistics battalion convoy that left daily. What they didn't say was that the convoy had not reached Beirut in three weeks because of ambushes.

Despite shelling on the hillsides, and stray small-arms fire, the convoy never stopped as we sped towards Beirut. The contrast from the sparkling Mediterranean with its turquoise waves, to Beirut itself, was startling. Garbage lined the coastal beaches. Broken-down and shattered shacks, burned-out cars, piles of rubble, earth mounds, and battle debris littered the area. Apartment blocks carried the scars of many battles. Rocket, cannon, and artillery impacts dotted everywhere.

Numerous detours were required before we reached our Beirut headquarters. We were not there five minutes when a tremendous explosion rocked the building. The Italian ammunition dump at the base of the hill had been hit by a round which sent the whole dump up with it.

At the exact moment of the explosion, I was grabbed by the shoulder and spun around a corner. I met for the first time another Canadian observer who was to become a very close friend. The building still shook as he calmly said, "I find this a good place to be in such circumstances." Captain Geordie Elms welcomed me to my new surroundings.

Although times were tough, some observers had

> "Unlike any wedding I'd ever seen," recalls Shirley Elms, of the marriage between an Australian with UNTSO in Beirut and his Christian Lebanese bride. "There were shell holes throughout the church. As it was nearly Christmas, they built a crèche out of old ammo boxes."

their wives with them in Beirut. With some persuasion, my fiancée agreed to come over as well. As Christmas was approaching, Jill wanted a Christmas tree. We bought a live one and our observer friends decorated it with whatever was handy, amusing or nationalistic.

After Christmas it was obviously dying, so I hauled it downstairs to throw it out. A group of teenagers worked in the apartment block. By day they were typical young men, but by night they were militiamen. They took the tree and planted it in front of the building.

For me, that was yet another reminder of the life and beauty evident throughout Lebanon. These young warriors, who had known only the horrors of war since birth, were planting this tree in hopes of rejuvenation not unlike their own hopes for the future.

Major Cook served with the UN Truce Supervision Organization, Observer Group Beirut, in 1983–84. He and Jill were married two years later.

A VERY TOUCHY SPOT

Major Vern McKeen

Lebanon

My first day on the job with the UN Truce Supervision Organization in Lebanon, I was robbed at gunpoint.

Two Americans, two Swedes, and I were being shown the route leading to the observation posts where the peacekeepers were working. We were unarmed, as all the observers were. You were actually much safer without a gun.

As we were being driven along the route we came around a bend. All of a sudden this fellow leaped from the bank. He had a balaclava pulled over his head and was pointing a Kalashnikov rifle at us. By gosh, this was for real!

We were motioned into an olive grove where another gunman was waiting. They hauled us out of the vehicle, stretched us out on the ground, and took our wallets.

A friend of mine had been picked up by gunmen in southern Lebanon a few years earlier, and his group had been stripped naked. I was hoping to hell these fellows didn't do that. Fortunately, they just took our money and buggered off. Welcome to Lebanon.

In fairness, most Lebanese had a very good attitude about Canadians. In fact, we were issued large flags to sew on our uniforms, to make it apparent exactly where we were from. Not everybody had that good fortune. After the gunmen left, the two Americans in our group told me they had had their hands over their flags, and one was trying to rip his off. They knew they were in a very touchy spot.

Part of our job was making contacts among the local people. We knew that one of the villages in our area was controlled by Hezbollah fighters, but we were having a tough time contacting them.

One day I was having tea with a young guy from the town, and he told me that he wished he could speak better English. A while later I happened across a little dictionary in a shop. I bought it and kept it with me. When I ran across this man again I gave it to him. He was so pleased, he called his friends over and introduced us. We got to chatting, and they all turned out to be members of the Hezbollah.

That little dictionary was a damned good investment. When the Hezbollah stepped up its campaign to plant mines along certain roadways, I found out about it – how the mines were put in place, the size of the explosives, where they got them, that sort of thing.

I reported what I'd learned. But we had no choice. We had to operate on those roads. It wasn't much later that Gilbert Côté hit a mine with his jeep.

It was a fascinating tour. I still bore people with the stories. I enjoyed what I was doing. I was a believer.

Major McKeen was an observer with the UN Truce Supervision Organization, monitoring ceasefire violations between Lebanon and Israel in 1987.

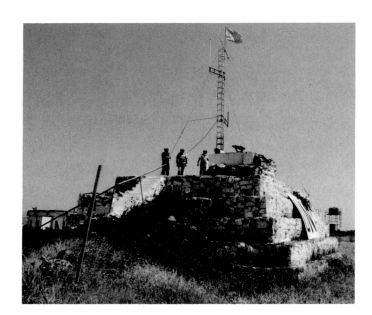

"We were unarmed, as all the observers were," says Major Vern McKeen, who manned UNTSO observation posts along the disputed Lebanese–Israeli border areas in 1987. "You were actually much safer without a gun."

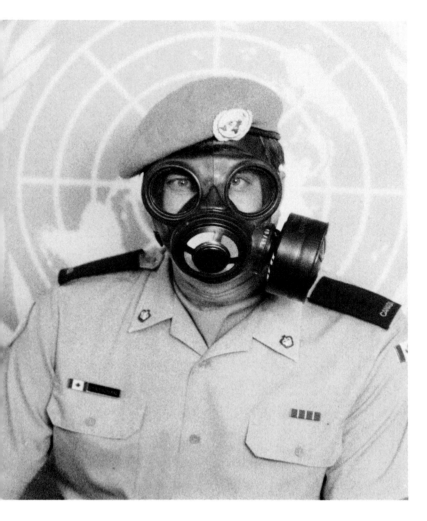

"Up in the Golan, just keeping the peace." Masked against the uncertain perils of SCUD missile attack during the Gulf War, an UNDOF Canlog officer faces the threats of germ and chemical warfare.

TOUR OF DUTY

OFFICERS OF CCUNDOF

Israel

When I am back home sometime later this year,
Some guy at some Legion will buy me a beer.
He'll ask what I did in the War in the Gulf.
This is the question I've been asking myself.

If you read in the papers 'bout the troops in Bahrain,
They'd have you believe that we missed the train.
Too far from the action to really be vets,
Just driving our trucks instead of fast jets.

The "human interest", it seems, was at Canada Dry One,
Where tensions were high 'neath the hot Arab sun.
So CBC News didn't get to the Heights,
To spend time in the shelters on SCUD-alert nights.

The flames of the war didn't come very near.
And maybe, just maybe, it's because we were here.
Just doing our jobs, day after day,
Unnoticed by most and for no danger pay.

I guess in peacekeeping there isn't much glory.
We didn't make the news as some feature story.
But we were here before those other guys came,
And I'll look at that guy who is buying me beer:
"Yes, I did my part in that War in the east;
I was up in the Golan, just keeping the peace."

*Written by officers serving with CCUNDOF – the
Canadian Contingent of UNDOF –– and published in the
Camp Ziouani Monthly Review, March 1991. Camp
Ziouani, located on the Golan Heights, houses
Canadians serving with the UN Disengagement
Observer Force.*

A CHAPLAIN'S VIEW

Captain Phil Morley

Iran–Iraq

It all happened very fast. I had just returned to Canada from a four-year tour of duty in Germany. I hadn't even really moved in. At the last minute they needed a chaplain as part of Canada's contribution to the Iran–Iraq mission. I was the one.

Going in, there were all sorts of concerns, about gassing, minefields, being westerners in an Islamic world. There was a lot of apprehension. I found people got very religious, very quickly.

I met this one fellow on the flight. He wanted baptism on the spot. I wanted him to think about what he was doing, so I gave him some Scriptures to read and promised that, when I came to his location, I would baptize him then.

I arrived one day, not realizing that was where he was stationed. Just as I was about to start my service he appeared. "Well, I'm ready, padre," he said. "Are you going to baptize me now?"

We had to think fast, and wound up using his shaving bowl for it. We baptized him right there, in the middle of the desert.

Besides offering worship and counselling, I would often give a padre's lecture on biblical lands. I'm very interested in archaeology, and some of the most ancient areas in the Scriptures are in the Iran–Iraq region. Like the cradle of civilization – by tradition, the Garden of Eden. The men were very interested. A lot of them had no idea where we were.

My services were open to all Christians. Canada was the only country to send a chaplain, so wherever I went Christian folk from many different nations would attend – Africans, Americans, even officers from behind the Iron Curtain. We usually had a very good turnout. Often 100 percent. The guys had no TVs or anything, and a lot of them were taking a look at the fervour of the Islamic religion over there, and taking a deeper look at their own beliefs.

It was quite an experience. Very rewarding.

Protestant chaplain Captain Morley served with the 1988 UN Iran–Iraq Military Observer Group.

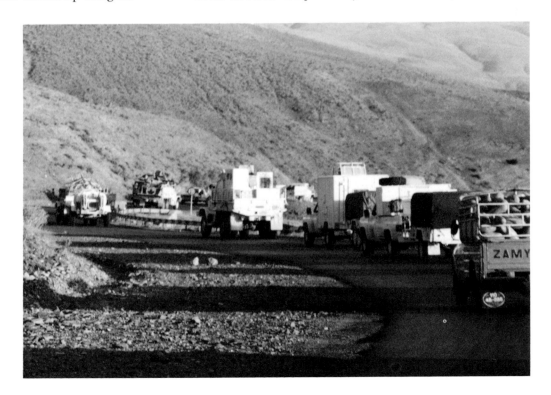

Snaking through the mountains separating Iran and Iraq, a UN convoy traverses lands of ancient biblical stories. As chaplain to the scattered groups of Canadians serving with UNIIMOG, Captain Morley found a lot of the soldiers re-examining their beliefs. "Being westerners in an Islamic world, people got very religious, very quickly."

COFFIN WARS

CAPTAIN BOB SCOTT

Iran–Iraq

On every mission I've been connected with, there has always been a requirement for somebody from the UN to oversee the exchange of bodies. In some cases they're quite a few years old. But with the Iran–Iraq operation the war had just ended, so the bodies were fairly fresh, if you will.

When the big day arrived, I'd be out there waiting in no man's land. It had to be a clear area where everybody could see everything through field glasses, so there could be no place to hide or sneak around. That was a big condition. We didn't want to get out into the middle and have a problem on our hands.

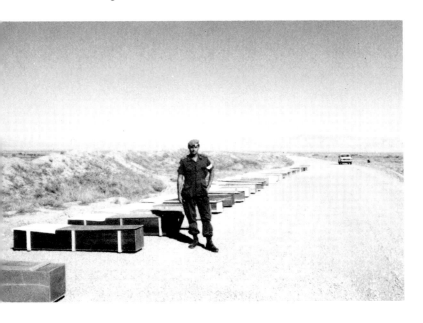

Alone in the company of the fallen, Captain Scott stands watch over a line of simple wooden coffins near the Iran–Iraq border. His white armband signifies an unarmed member of a UNIIMOG body-exchange party.

Initially, trucks would pull up loaded with bodies simply rolled in blankets. That was really, really horrible. But as time went by, the exchanges became a little more humane. The UN started insisting on some form of coffin. There's not a lot of wood in the Middle East, but they could build plywood boxes. That was something. It was sure better for us. They were easier to transport and it looked a lot better.

It sounds awful; it *was* awful. Maybe it didn't seem so bad at the time because *everything* was kind of awful.

Toward the end they actually began to decorate the coffins. They got into elaborate coffin wars then, one side trying to outdo the other. One would put a few branches on their coffins, and say, "See all the trouble we go to? And they do nothing for our dead." Next time we'd do an exchange, the others would have branches *plus* flags painted on the coffins. In a situation like that, you're dealing with a lot of emotions. People aren't always entirely rational.

It was fairly emotional. They'd usually hold a little ceremony right on the spot. They'd pray for a couple of minutes, load up, and leave. While they were in the middle we'd make them sign for what they were getting, just so nobody could accuse anyone else of failing to deliver. It was an elaborate procedure, and as soon as you figured you had all the angles covered, one side or the other would pop up with the problem of the day. You didn't want to be stuck out in the middle when that happened.

We had one particular case, one of the sides looked at a coffin that was being delivered and said, "We don't want this one. It's not one of ours." I had to be real firm. They sure weren't leaving it with me. I couldn't do anything with it. What would you do if you got stuck with one and the others wouldn't take it back? That was my biggest fear. It wasn't a lot of fun out there.

Captain Scott served as a military observer with the first contingent of UN forces in Iran–Iraq in 1988.

SOUVENIR DIPLOMACY

CAPTAIN GORDON RAMSAY

Kuwait

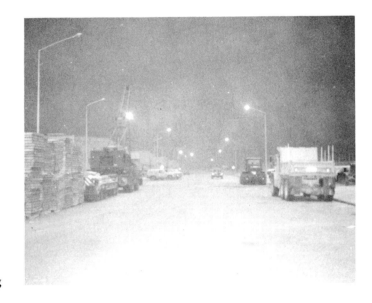

As we landed in Kuwait shortly after the war with Iraq had ended, my view from the aircraft window was unforgettable. We could see the oil fires burning from miles away. As we descended through the thick veil of smoke, we could make out the heavy damage: craters in the runway, the control tower destroyed.

For the first month or so we were almost constantly smoked in. It would hang up in the atmosphere, blocking the sun. At high noon the sun would be nothing more than an orange disc faintly visible through the smoke. Some days were totally black, just like midnight. You'd sneeze or blow your nose, and the Kleenex would be covered in black stuff.

My job was paying the soldiers, liaising with local suppliers, and keeping accounts. I located a bank that was still open, but I found it frustrating adjusting to their way of doing business. In Canada, if you stand in line at a bank teller you expect to be served in turn; over there it's no guarantee at all. It was more like mass confusion.

I soon caught on to something interesting. In the Middle East, gifts are a big deal, especially coming from a non-Arab. Dealing with suppliers, for example, I learned that a case of Coke or a carton of Canadian cigarettes could go a long way toward smoothing out procurement problems.

It was the same at the bank. Every time I had to visit the manager I would make a point of taking along a small gift of some kind – a desk flag, collar pins with the Canadian maple leaf. When I saw how much those were appreciated, I phoned my wife and asked her to get me some souvenir coffee mugs from Banff. She also sent over one of those little glass bubbles filled with liquid that you shake to make a snowy winter scene. It was from our home town, Newcastle, New Brunswick. Marwan, the bank manager, just loved it. From that time

Kuwait City, 10:00 a.m. Streetlights burn day and night as well-fires set by retreating Iraqis during the Gulf War spew immense clouds of oily smoke. "Some days were totally black, just like midnight," says Captain Ramsay. "You'd sneeze or blow your nose and the Kleenex would be covered in black stuff."

on I found myself waiting less to make transactions.

I did the same with Furad, the foreign-exchange manager. Whenever I went in, there would always be four or five foreigners waiting around his desk. I would walk up in my uniform and Furad would say, "Mr. Ramsay. Good to see you. Would you like a cup of tea?" He'd slide through the crowd and say to the others, "Excuse me. Mr. Ramsay is very busy. I have to serve him immediately."

I was there to support the troops. Being sensitive to local custom and being a bit of a diplomat improved service and gave me a higher probability of getting the job done. It was one of those things you have to learn as you go, nothing you could pick up in a book.

Captain Ramsay was finance officer for the first Canadian contingent to the 1991 UN Iraq–Kuwait Observation Mission.

CHILDREN OF THE DESERT

CAPTAIN RAY LALANDE
Kuwait–Iraq

Whenever I think back on the mission to Kuwait, I remember the children. Along the demilitarized zone where we were working, you'd see kids without shoes or proper clothing, sometimes without even underwear, just their torn, dirty T-shirts. They were running around like that out in the desert, begging for food and water.

The whole area was a mess: blown-up buildings and cars, roads all torn up, electrical poles knocked down, trucks and tanks littering the desert. But most of all I noticed the children. I have a little girl, Valery. You can't help thinking of your family when you're in a place like that.

For part of the time we were located near Umm Qasr in Iraq, clearing routes of mines and explosives. There were farms all around, and they had been bombed and shelled by the Allied forces when the Iraqi army was occupying the area. It was infested with unexploded ordnance.

The first couple of days we noticed the kids watching us. Whenever we'd blow a mine, we'd first have to make sure the kids were in a secure area or else take them home. After a while they decided they wanted to help too. These kids knew where to find mines. They began picking them out of their fields and bringing them to us. Live mines! They could go off at any instant.

The first thing you wanted to do was to grab the mines away from them, but that was dangerous too. For them and for us. We could only communicate through sign language – pointing, making noises. We'd finally get them to lay the mines down gently and walk away. Five minutes later they'd be back with more.

The stuff was everywhere. People were getting hurt all the time. Even civilian engineers doing clearance were being injured, and they were qualified for the job. You can imagine what it was like for a Bedouin nomad or a child walking around out there.

It was serious work. Every single week I'd go over the security factors with my men. We couldn't afford to get cocky. I'd show them accident reports from other contingents. Every job had to be done professionally. I didn't want to be the one calling somebody's parents, telling them, "We've had an accident with your son."

Leaving Canada was tough. The hardest thing was saying goodbye to my wife and daughter. Valery was only thirteen months old. She didn't understand what was happening. She was just starting to speak when I left. A few months into the tour, on one of my phone calls home – we each got ten minutes a week – she was saying words, saying, "Papa." I wish I'd been there when she said Papa for the first time.

Captain Lalande returned to Canada in the spring of 1992 after a six-month tour with the UN Iraq–Kuwait Observation Mission.

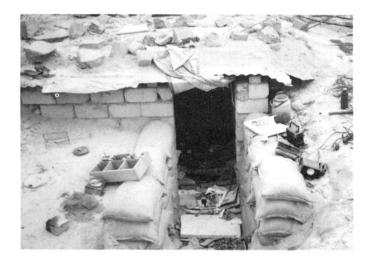

Abandoned in a hasty retreat, this deserted Iraqi trench system constructed in Kuwait during the Gulf War still holds ammunition and supplies. "The fields were infested with unexploded ordnance," says Captain Lalande. "You can imagine what it was like for a Bedouin child walking around out there."

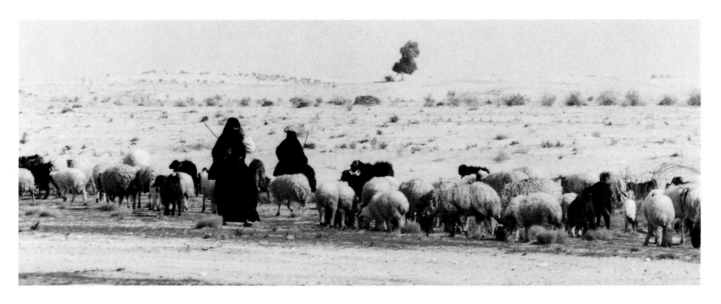

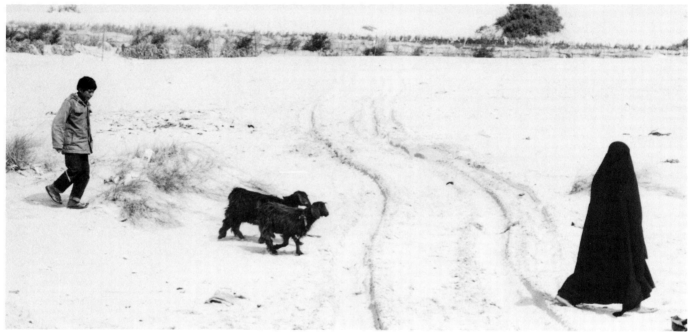

Bedouin shepherds tend
their flocks. Notice the
deeply rutted tire tracks.
"When there's a sand-
storm and it starts
raining," says Capt.
Robert Benson, "it turns
into a mud storm. If
you're out there you get
covered. There are lots
of surprises."

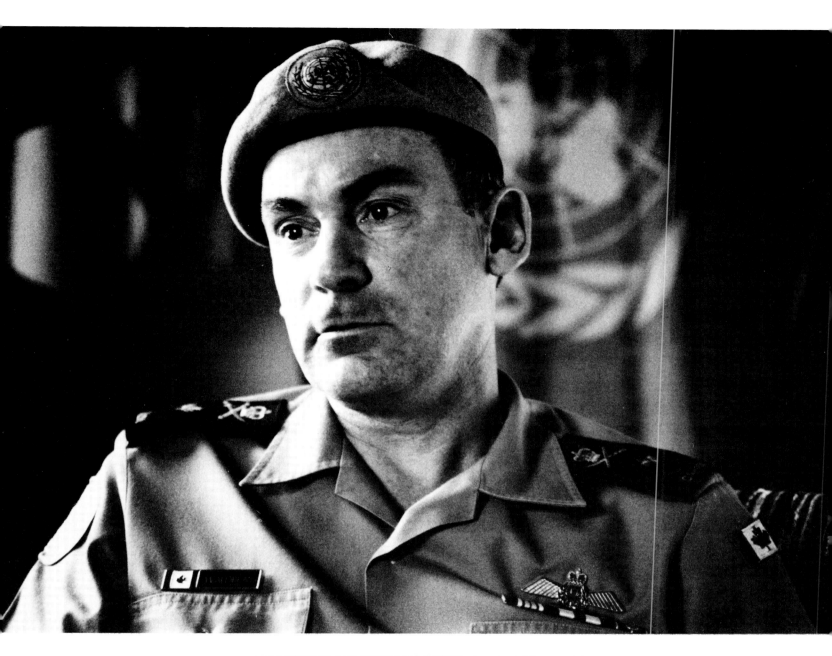

ABOVE:
"As a world citizen, Canada is obligated to provide the resources at its command," says UNDOF Chief of Staff Brig.-Gen. Butch Waldrum. "We have a role to play in limiting the tremendous damage wars inflict – here in the Middle East and wherever we can contribute to peace."

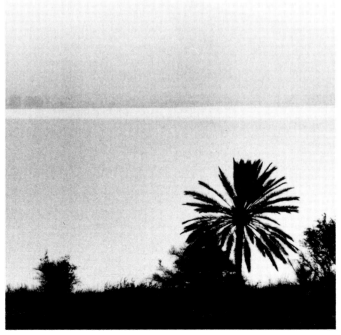

LEFT:
The strategically important Golan Heights – seen here across the Sea of Galilee – rise from gently rolling hills to snow-covered Mount Hermon.

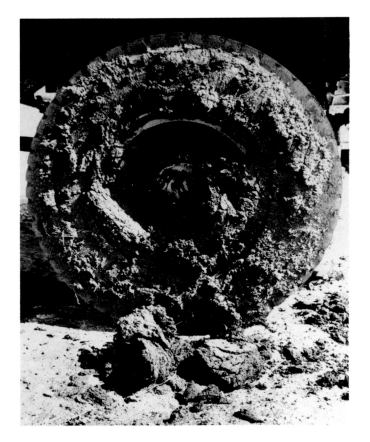

"Tough going" in the Golan Heights is not restricted to a political context. The snow, mud, rocks, and rough terrain make servicing the camp's vehicles an ongoing challenge for maintenance personnel like Cpl. Jack Beauregard.

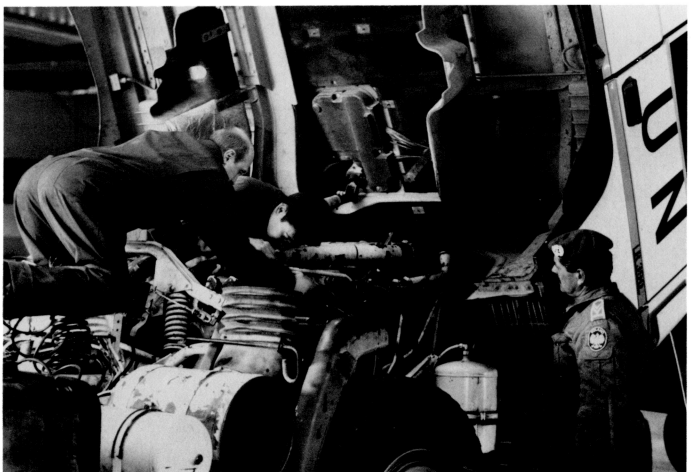

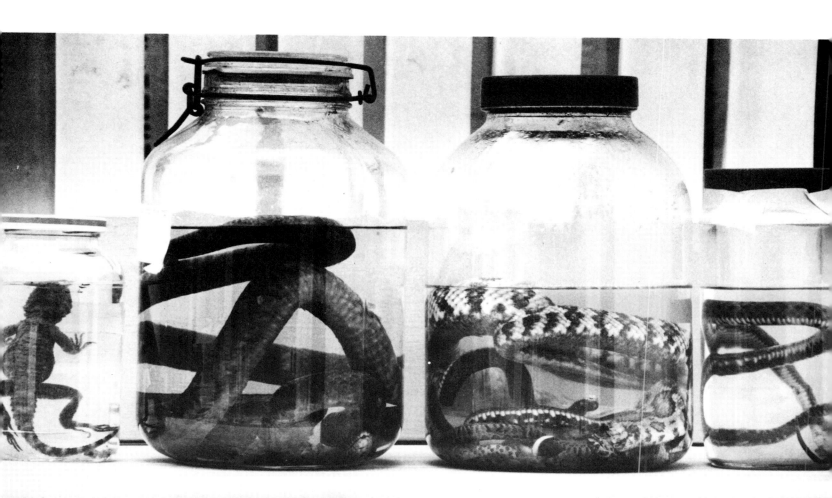

The casualties treated by the medical team at Camp Ziouani have suffered more natural hazards than military ones. Palestinian vipers, black rat snakes, and scorpions are but three members of the poisonous menagerie native to the Golan Heights.

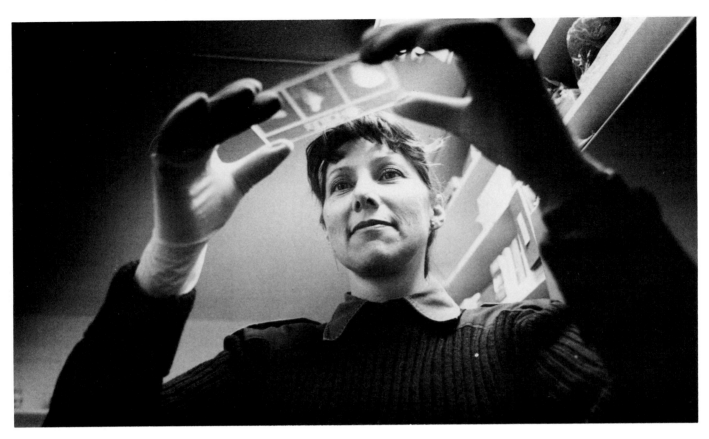

With medical assistants like M/Cpl. Ben Moran and Sgt. Helen Martin in the pharmacy, the infirmary deals with all but the most serious injuries. Although the base is stationed just 100 metres from Israeli troops and 300 metres from the Syrians, virtually no shots have been fired along the disputed border in the 16 years UNDOF has been positioned between the two nations.

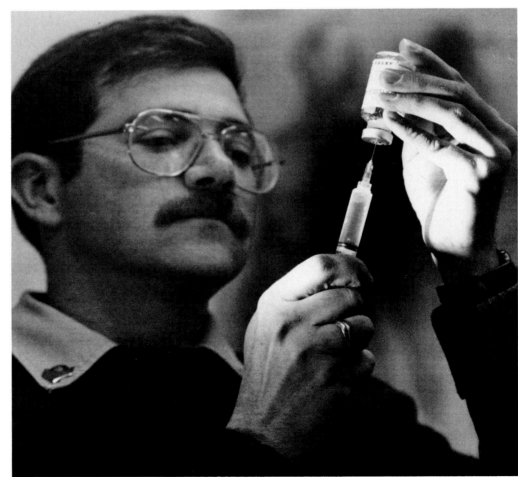

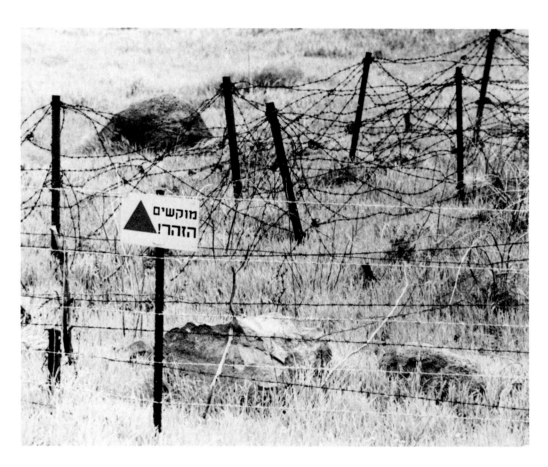

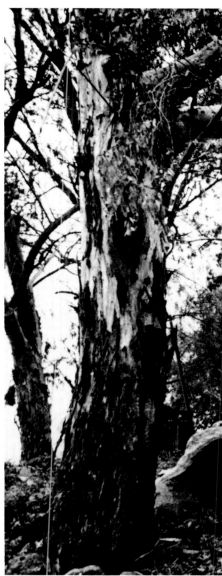

Legacy of two wars, minefields on the Golan Heights pose some unusual problems. Grass fires, whipped by the wind, travel quickly here, to the crump of detonating mines. So until a fire reaches the cleared area immediately surrounding a UNDOF outpost position, troops dare not fight it.

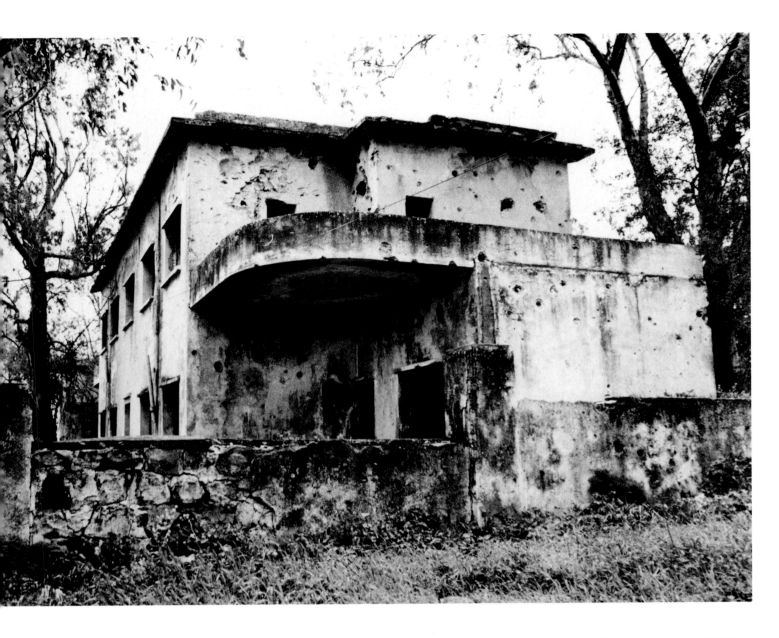

Battle scars of the 1967
Six Day War and the 1973
Yom Kippur War mar
Syrian villages.

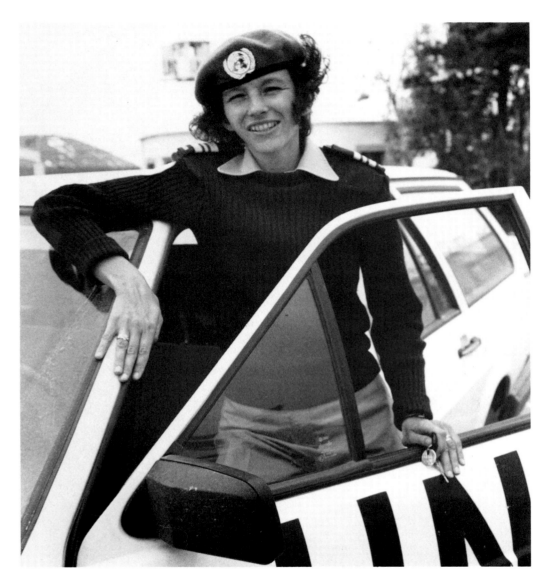

Maj. Marie Leloup heads off base for the long trip into Tiberias. "You can't go anywhere on foot or bike, and you can't call a taxi," says Capt. Guy Desrochers. "You absolutely need a vehicle. And a full tank of gas."

A local Israeli barber employed by the base administers a trim and some regulation moustache management.

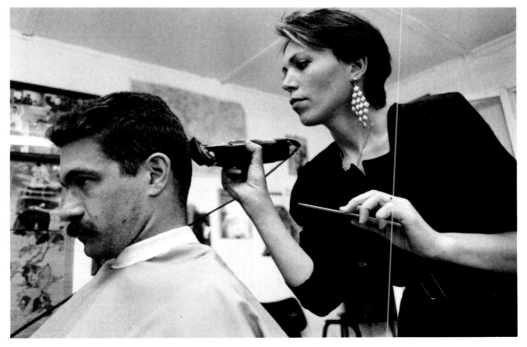

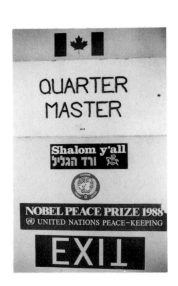

Busy crossroad for an army of stores, the quartermaster barracks under Sgt. Denis Guillemette coordinates supplies from spare parts to sand bags.

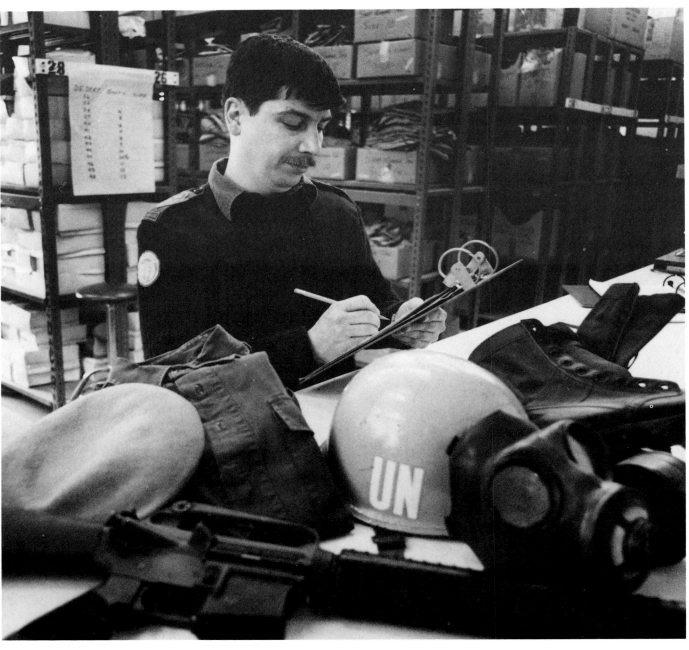

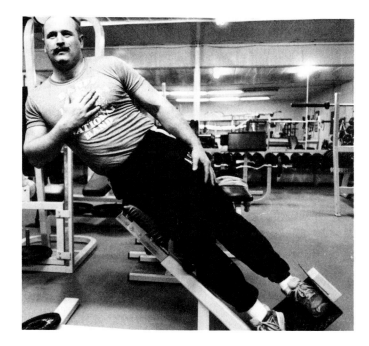

Shaping up, M/Cpl. Robert Darroch keeps trim in the Camp Ziouani gym. Running is also popular, but in this mine-strewn land joggers stick to the roads.

With the resort town of Tiberias a popular recreation run, paymaster M/Seaman Darrel Colley is kept busy providing personnel with draws on their salary.

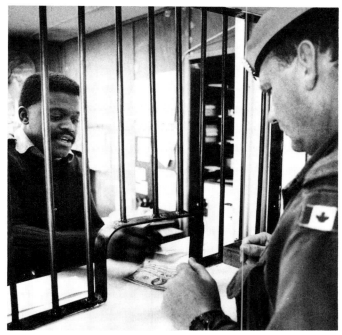

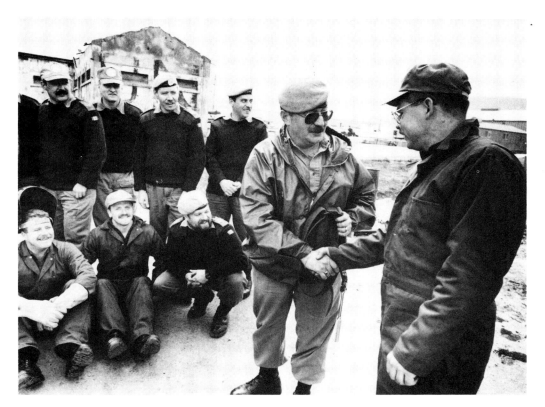

Lost keys, broken winches, 5-ton recovery trucks buried up to their axles – Sgt.-Maj. Philip Hughes and his crew of maintenance engineers have heard it all. Every week the biggest "klutz" is officially recognized. It's a distinction very few of the engineers manage to avoid during their 6-month tour.

His 6-month tour with UNDOF at an end, Captain Guy Desrochers finds his memories as tough to sort through as his kit. "Being here has given me the ability to step back, to look at things in a global way," he says. "I've learned a lot about myself."

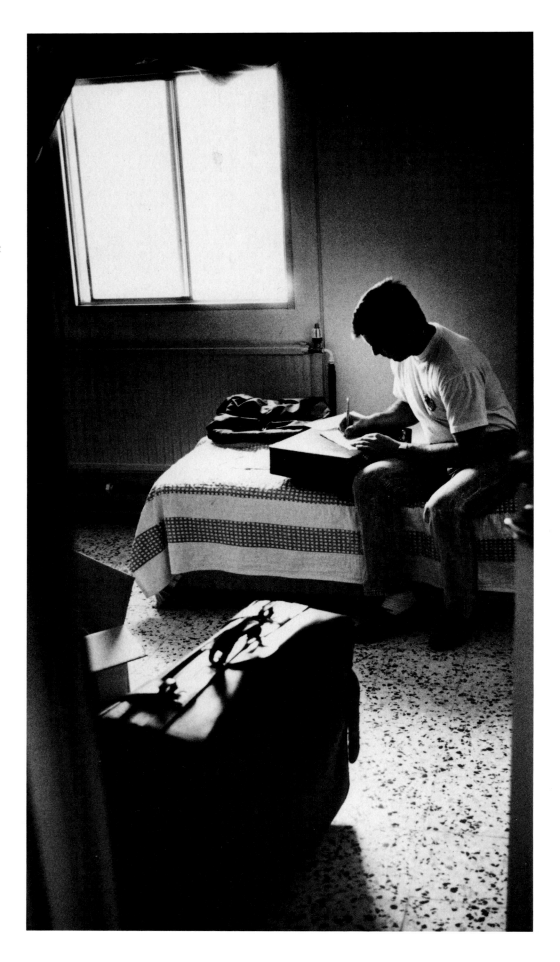

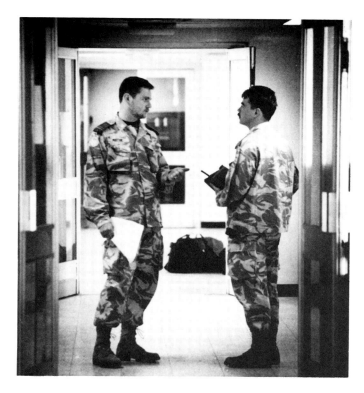

Sheltered from the blazing sun and blowing sand outside, Capt. Nicholas El Daoud holds an impromptu hallway conference with a UNIKOM colleague. The air-conditioned comfort of Canada's Doha base, actually a large factory warehouse, is a recent improvement. Earlier arrivals stoically resigned themselves to the building's unrelenting heat and inch-thick dust.

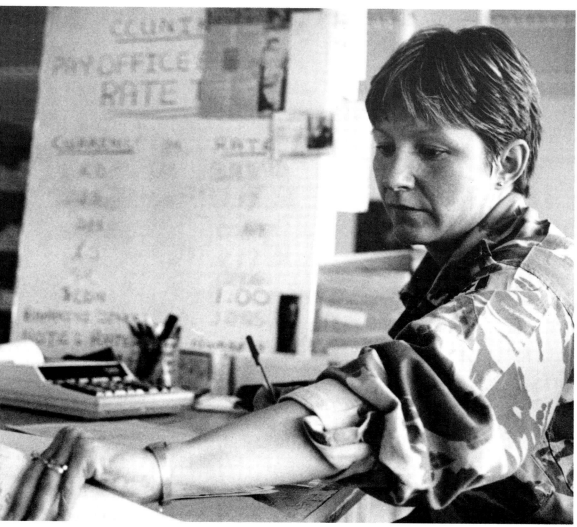

Pay records at one hand and adding machine at the other, peacekeepers in the paymaster's office offer cash *and* counselling. Because printing plates were stolen by invading Iraqis, the design of Kuwaiti bank notes was changed after the war. Canadian personnel had to learn to distinguish the new legal tender from discontinued or counterfeit bills.

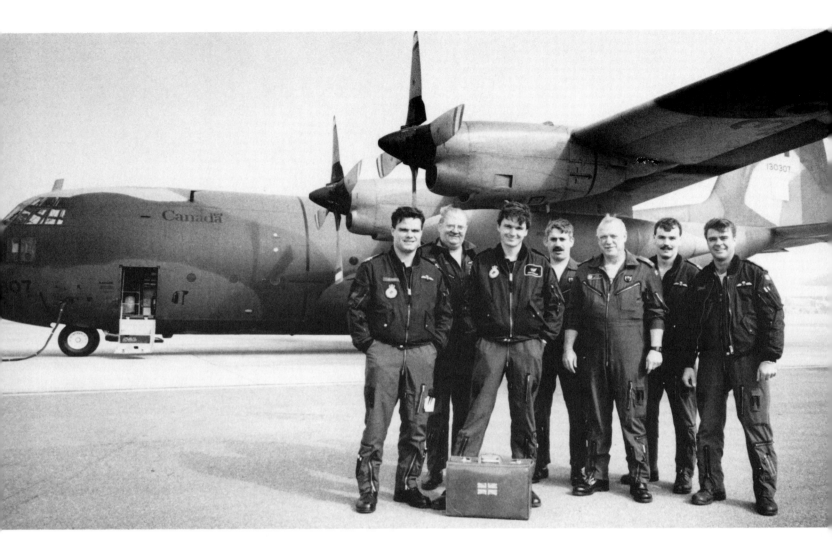

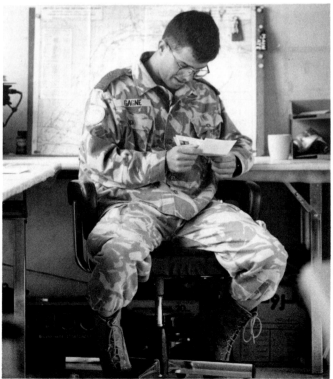

ABOVE:

Special delivery. The crew of a Hercules drops off supplies and picks up UNIKOM mail bound for home. Horror stories about lost and misrouted mail sent by commercial carriers make Canadian Forces flights a welcome alternative. "It's not very funny," says Postmaster Gaétan Lortie. "If people don't get their letters, you feel really bad."

No news from home is as thoroughly read and re-read as the mail a peace-keeper receives halfway around the world. Cpl. Stephane Gagné, in Doha, Kuwait, catches up on the latest family happenings back in Bromont, Quebec, in a letter from his sister.

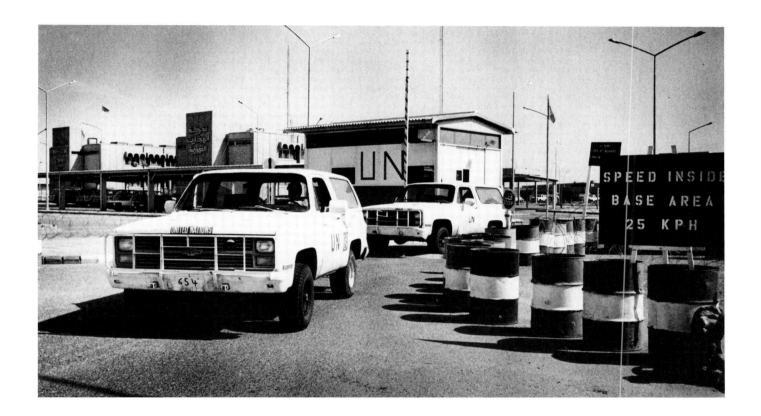

Leaving the confines of
the Doha base means
entering a world where
Arab habits, not Western
ones, prevail. It took some
time, says Sgt. Steve
Lovett, before he got used
to the driving habits of
the local community. "But
before long I knew Kuwait
City like the back of my
white-knuckled hand."

OPPOSITE:
"Logging the desert." Sgt.
Reynald Tremblay exer-
cises a skill more familiar
to his native Matane,
Quebec, than to the
scrub land of Iraq. Here
he clears a path at Camp
Khor on the Kuwait–Iraq
border.

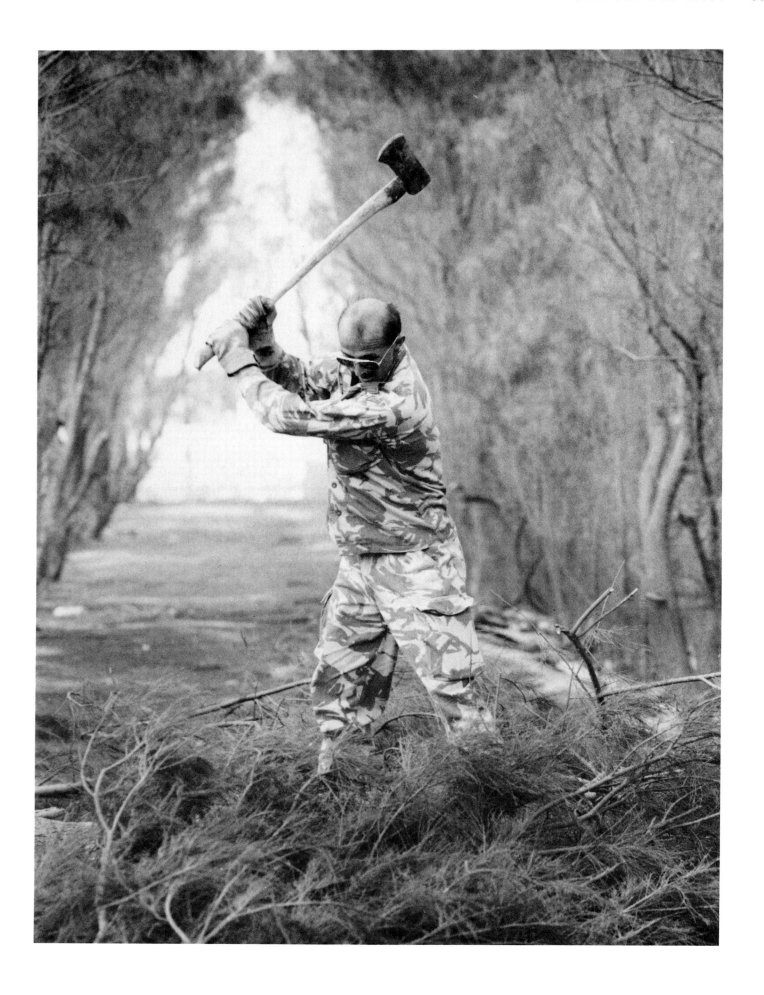

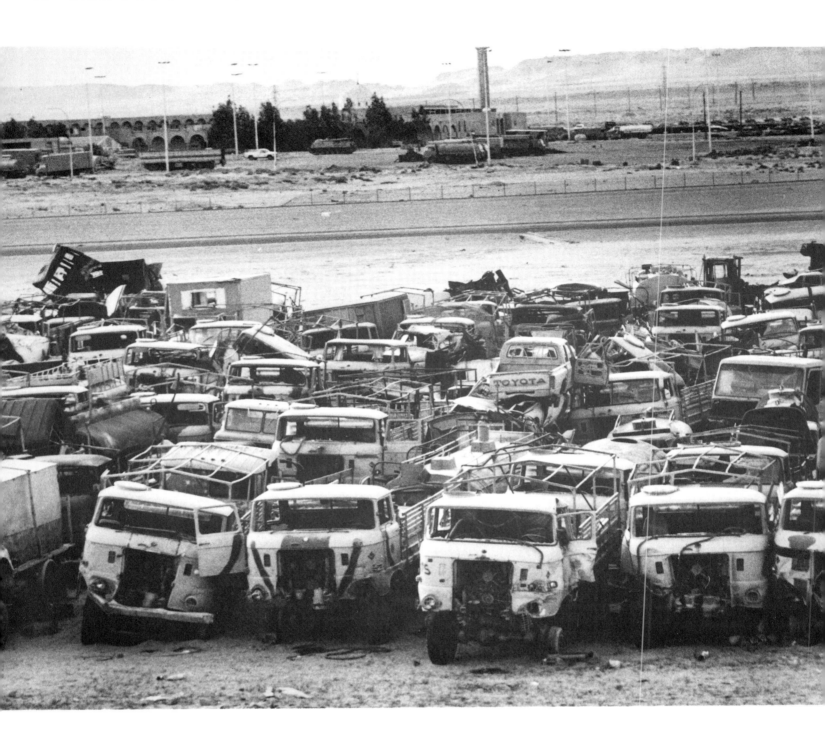

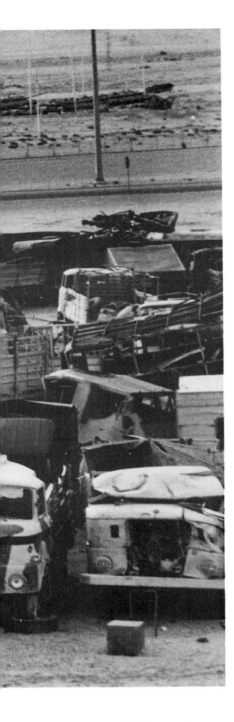

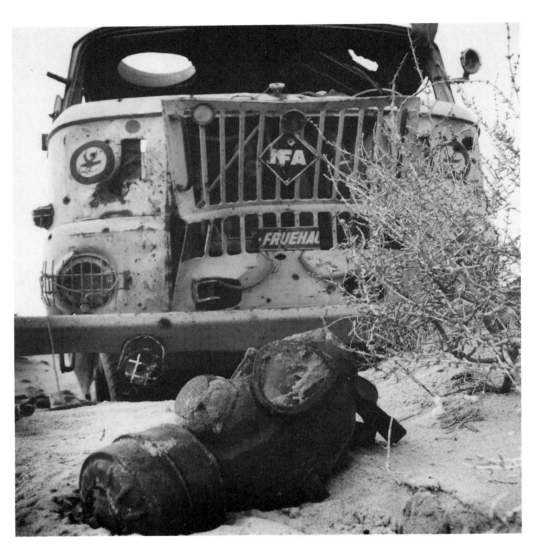

A story of defeat and horror lies already partly buried in the sand of the Kuwaiti desert – armoured vehicles stopped in their tracks by anti-tank helicopter attack, blown inside-out by heat-seeking missiles of the allied forces, signalling the last gasp of the evacuating Iraqis.

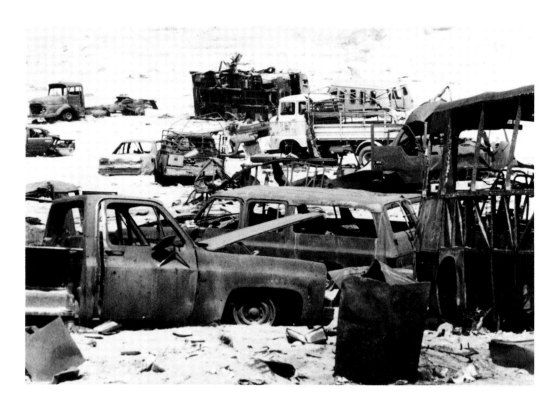

Fleeing vehicles were easy targets for allied armed forces on the "Highway to Hell".

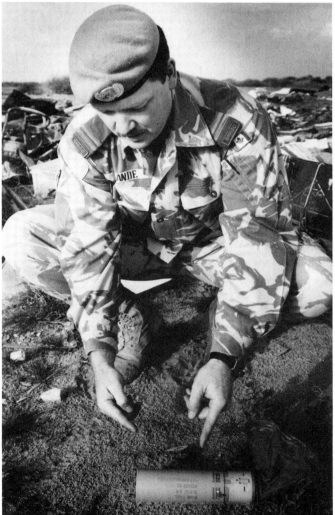

Capt. Ray Lalande points to an unexploded "bomblet" among the remains of a burned-out Iraqi vehicle in the Kuwait desert.

OPPOSITE:
Lethal leftovers of an abandoned arsenal. M/Cpl. Marc Bedard briefs newcomers on unexploded ordnance they may encounter in the Kuwait–Iraq demilitarized zone. "You think about your family every day," says Bedard. "But you have to draw a line. Especially in my job, I have to concentrate on what I'm doing."

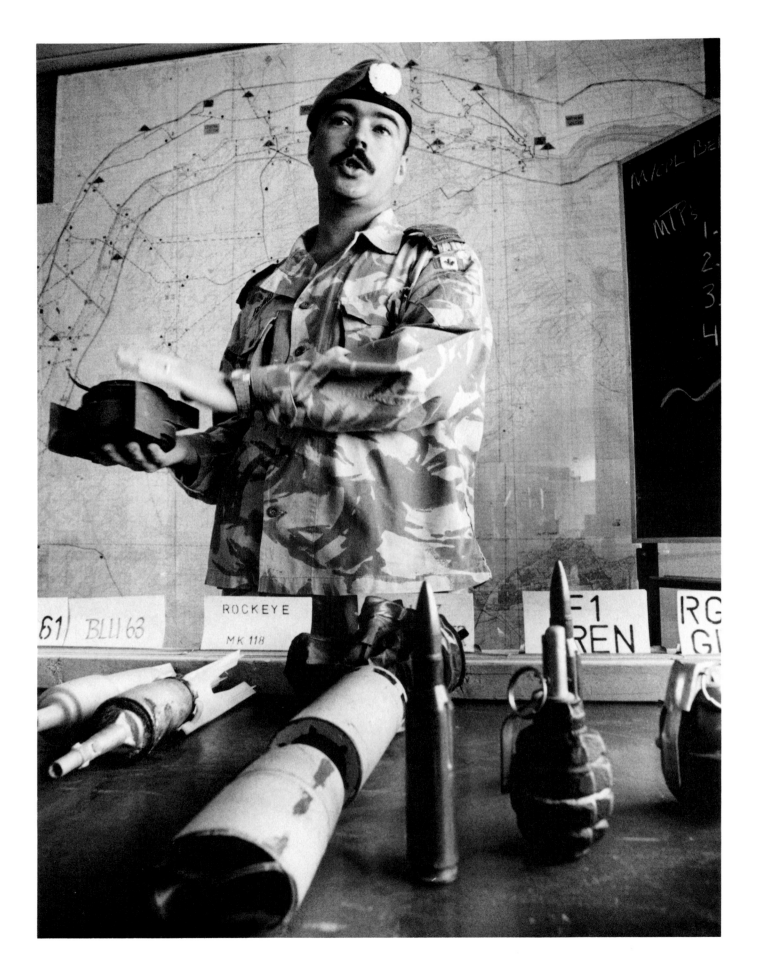

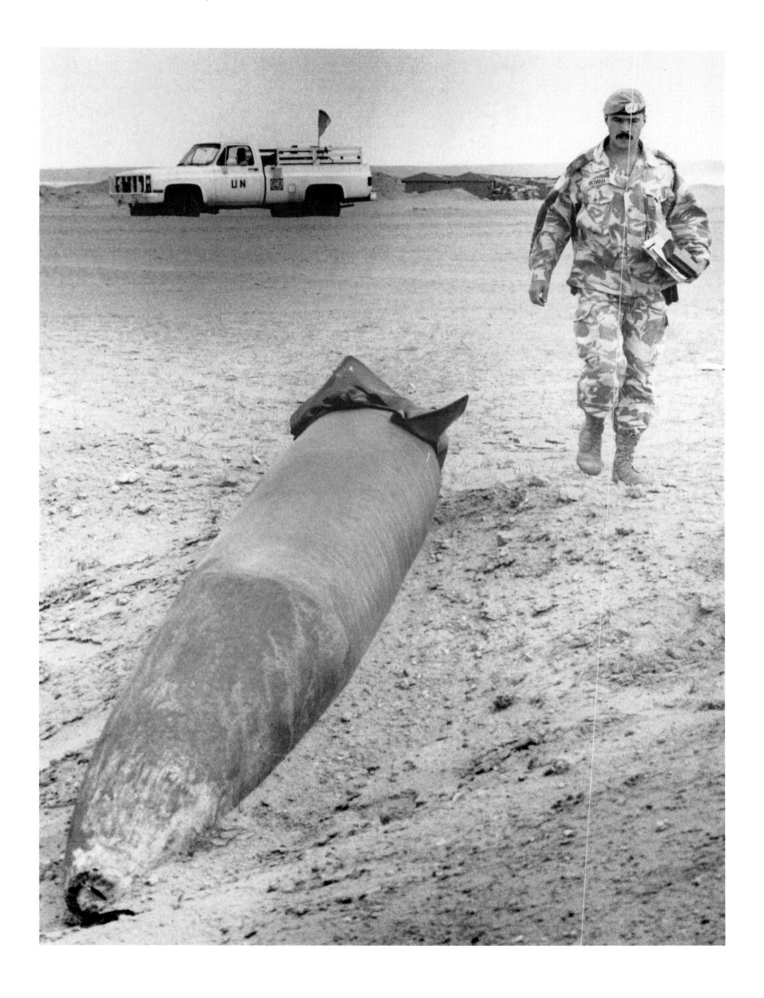

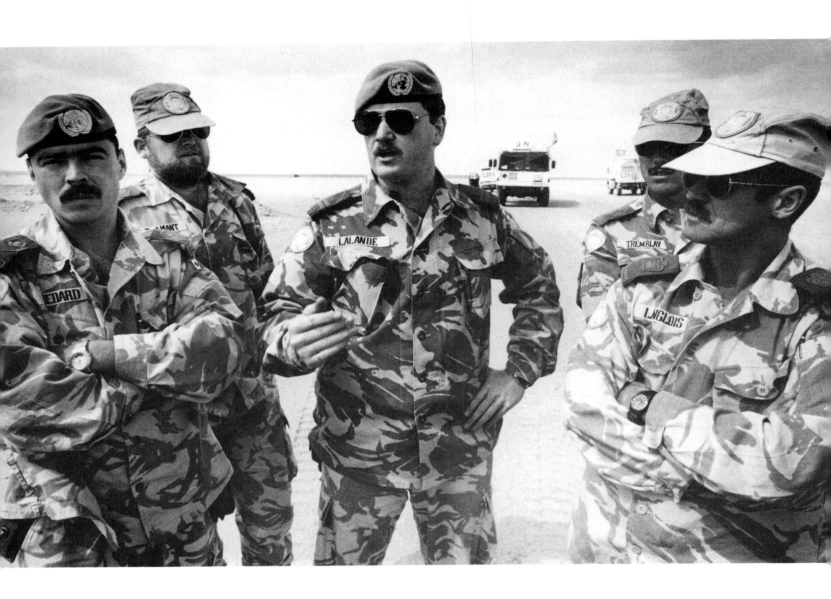

OPPOSITE:

Camera in hand, scanning the ground ahead for bomblets, M/Cpl. Bedard picks his way towards an unexploded 2,000-pound bomb. "A lot of things go through your mind. If that bomb goes off, you're history." After a thorough recce, he will photograph and mark the bomb so other members of the section can tell exactly what and where it is.

ABOVE:

The section team refines their strategy for neutralizing the 2,000-pound bomb. "Every single week I show my men the Accident and Incident Reports," says leader Capt. Ray Lalande. "After a couple of weeks you get cocky. We can't afford that. No Canadians at all have been injured so far – touch wood."

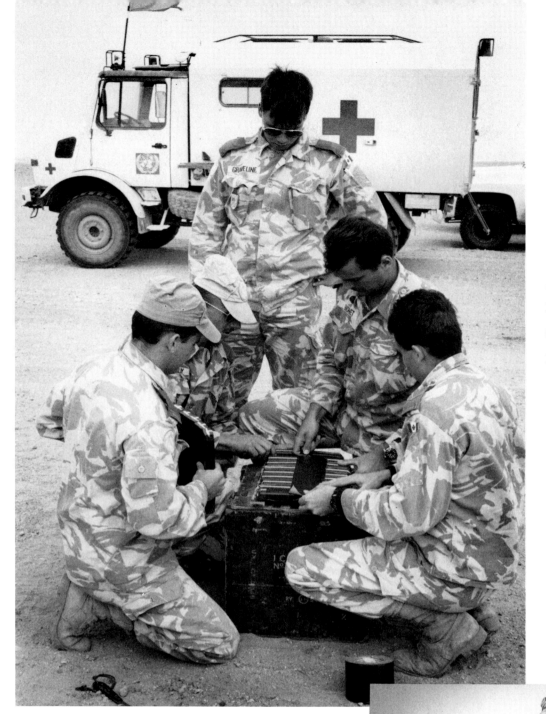

An explosive charge will detonate the bomb. "You don't want to get too confident about it," acknowledges M/Cpl. Bedard. "But you know what it is and you know what to do." First though, roads have to be blocked and nearby operation checkpoints evacuated.

Aftermath – a shred of metal from the detonated 2,000-pounder.

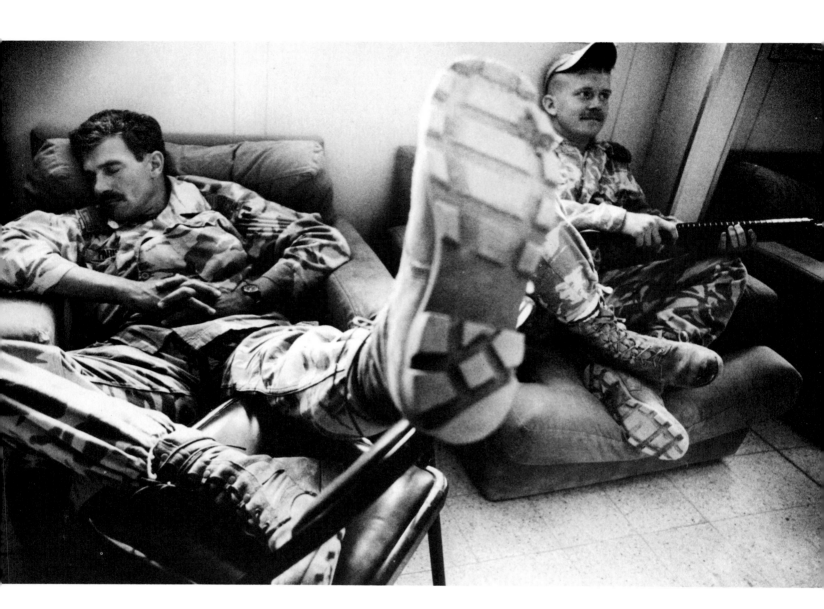

Bone-weary from hard,
hot hours clearing the
demilitarized zone, Sgt.
Conrad Parise falls into
an exhausted sleep.
"My job is to make sure
nothing goes wrong,"
says Capt. Lalande. "I
don't want to be the one
calling somebody's
parents, telling them,
'We've had an accident
with your son.' "

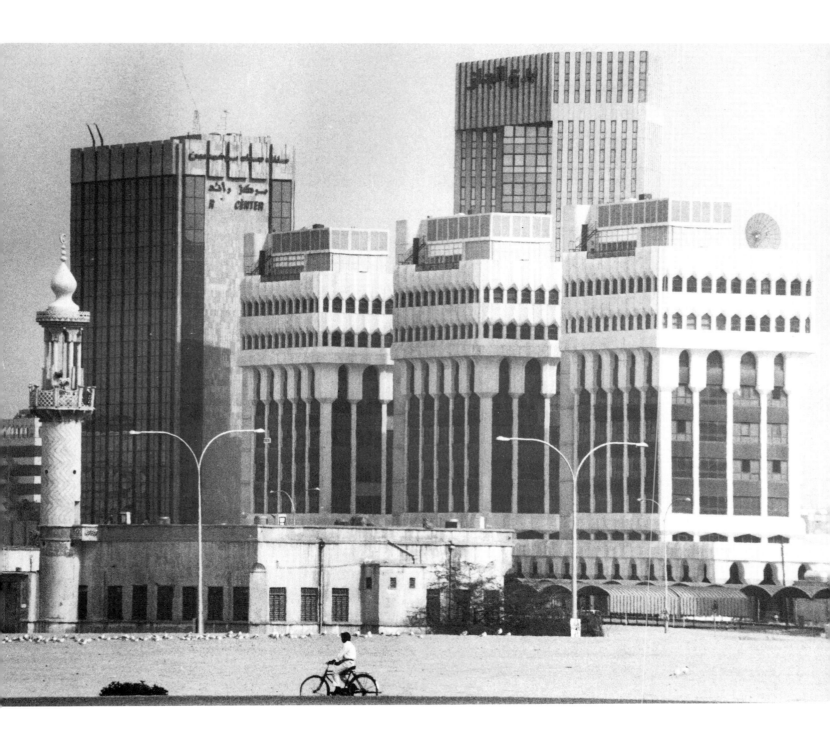

Downtown Kuwait City.

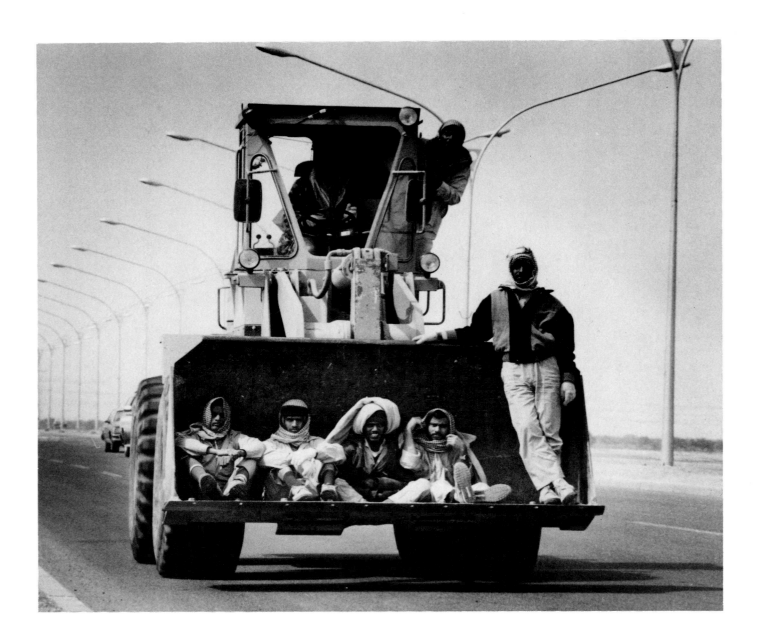

Guest workers join the enormous undertaking of restoring Kuwait to its pre-war condition. Recalls Sgt. Steve Lovett of his first trip from the airport to Doha: "We pounded over holes in the road left by coalition air strikes. The ride was an experience. I was occasionally bounced off the truck seat."

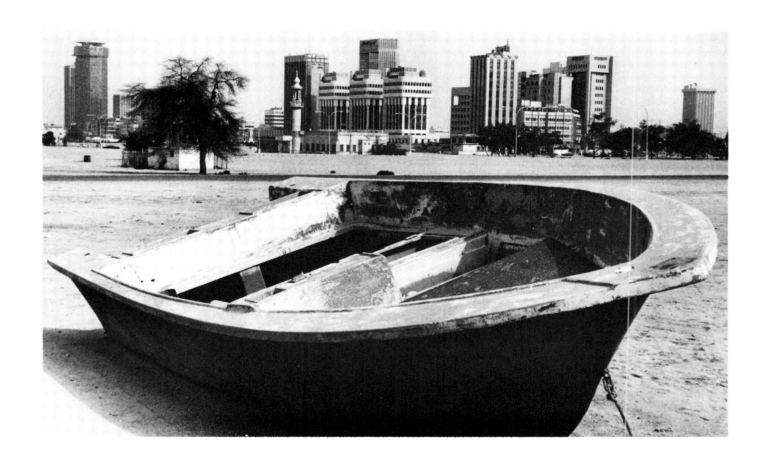

A forlorn fixture on an off-limits beach, an old boat lies in the sun. Despite the temptations of sand and sea, Muslim tradition prohibits sunbathing, or public exposure of any kind, on Kuwait City's sandy shore.

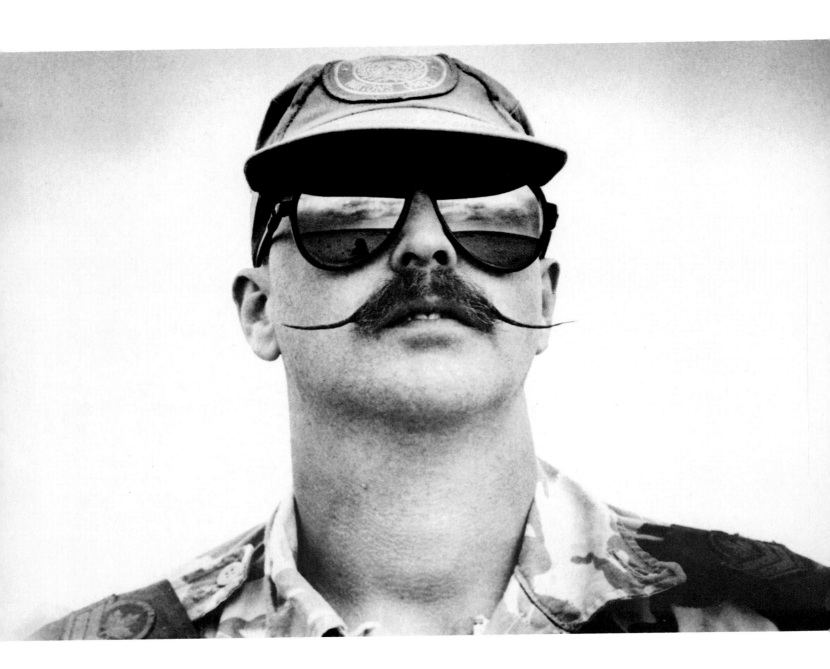

Kuwait offers Canadians like M/Cpl. Rich Carbonneau fresh insights into the job of peacekeeping. Says fellow UNIKOM soldier Diane Comeau, "It's not an eight-to-four job. When you're in a country that has been at war you never know what's going to happen. The stress really wears you down."

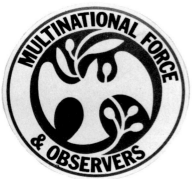

Emblem of harmony, the dove on the MFO crest symbolizes the force's peace-seeking mandate. Because the Soviet Union refused to support the force, a product of the 1979 U.S.-brokered Camp David Accord, it had to be set up outside UN auspices. Canada joined the operation in 1986.

Fortified against the unlikely but conceivable threat of extremist action, the MFO camp – home to 2,000 peacekeepers – is located on an abandoned Israeli air force base originally called Eitam.

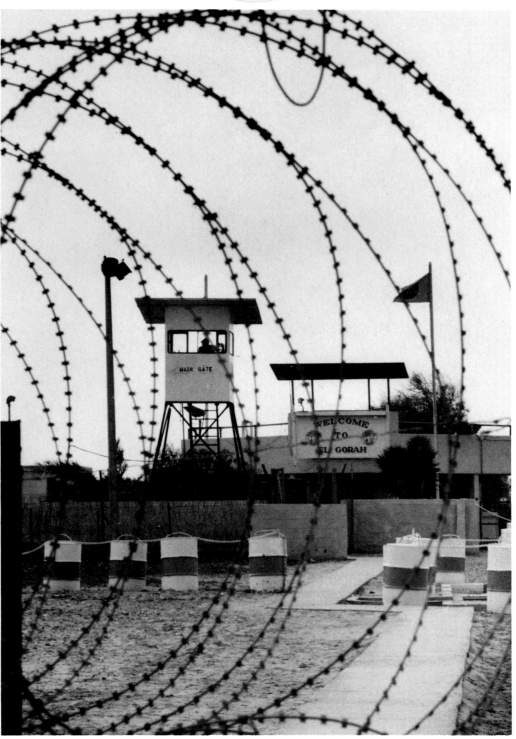

OPPOSITE:
A hub of activity in a largely barren desert, the main MFO base at El Gorah is the maintenance and refuelling centre for the force's helicopters. The aircraft overfly Egyptian and Israeli installations to verify that treaty limits on military personnel and armaments are not exceeded.

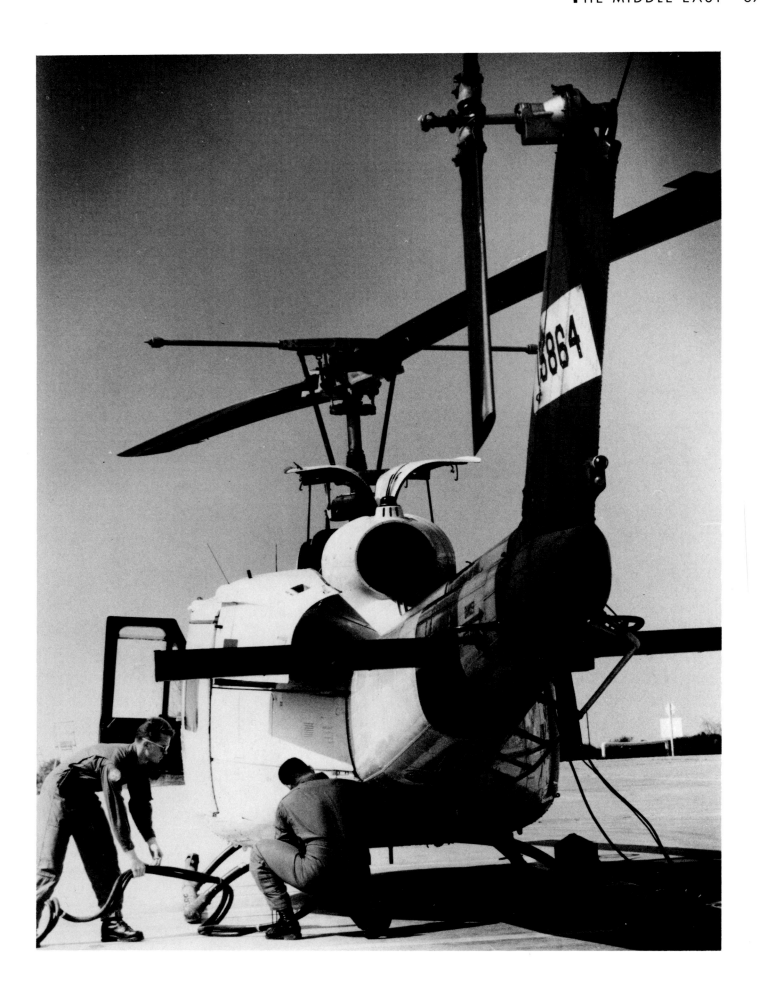

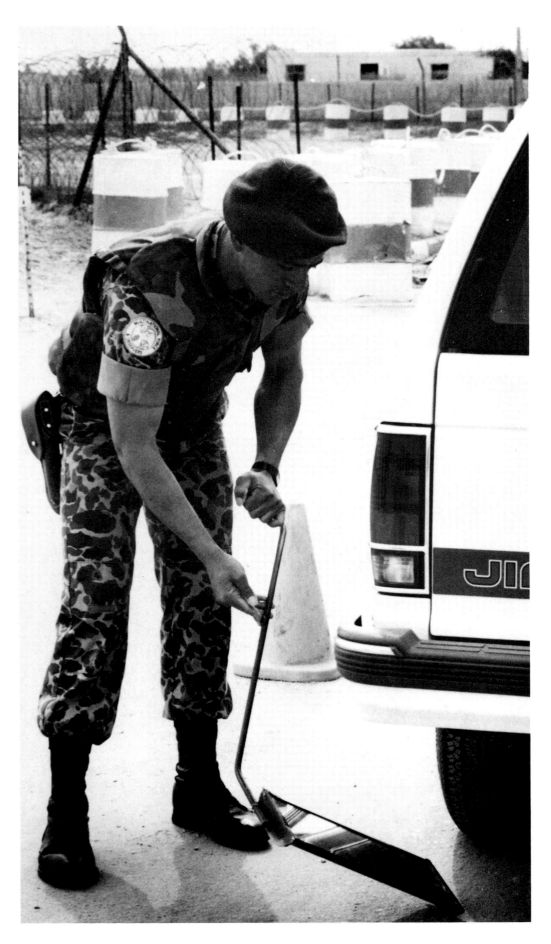

Inspecting the under-carriage of vehicles entering the El Gorah base, a Colombian soldier leaves nothing to chance. "My favourite part of the mission is the multicultural aspect," says Canadian Capt. Robert Benson. "You learn to say hello in ten different languages."

Wary hosts, Egyptian soldiers monitor vehicle and UN troop movements on roads leading to the El Gorah base. The continued success of the MFO relies entirely on Egyptian and Israeli support.

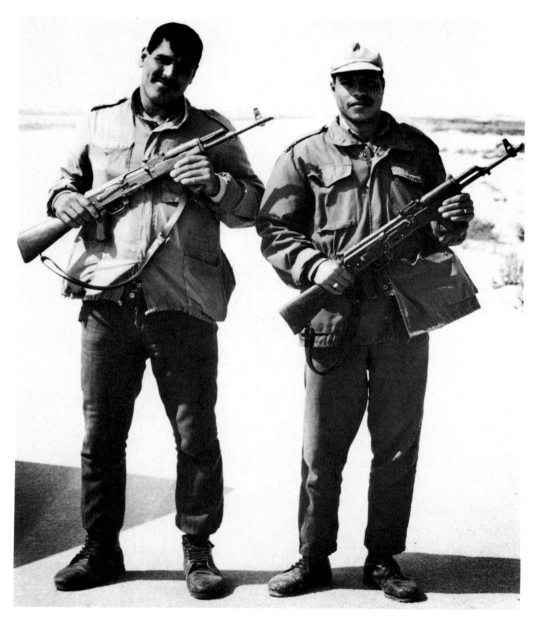

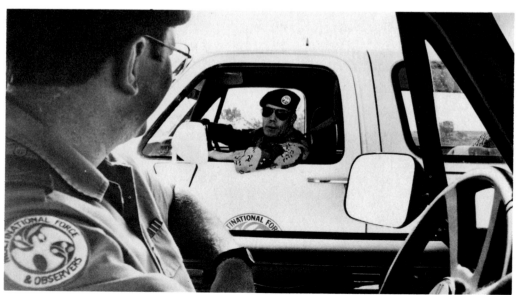

A quick update from a Colombian peacekeeper keeps a Canadian team member abreast of developments in the El Gorah area. "Our contingent is comfortable dealing at the international level," notes another Canadian, Col. William Rooke. "Canadians are an important bit of the glue."

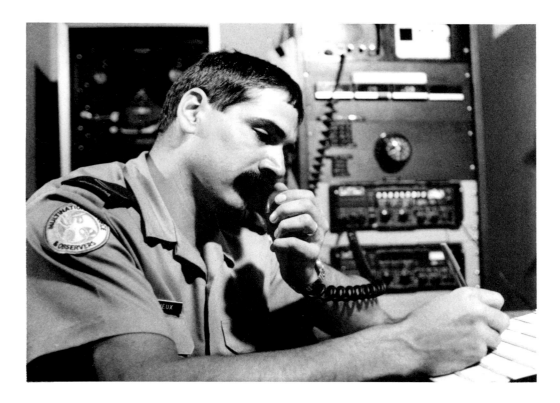

Flight-following is Canada's main contribution to MFO. Controllers like Cpl. Steve Lemieux chart the progress of aircraft leaving El Gorah for Sinai Desert airspace. If they don't report in within three minutes of their estimated time of arrival, a communications check is initiated. If no response is raised within 10 minutes, a search-and-rescue operation is mounted.

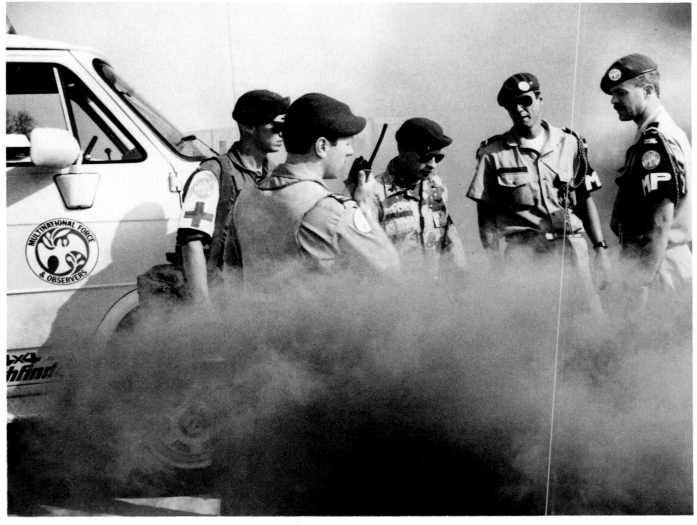

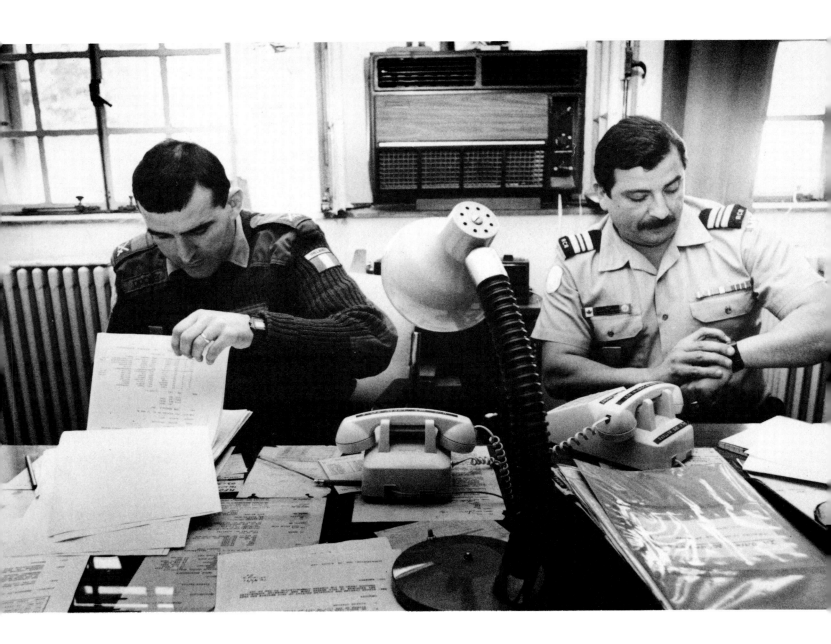

OPPOSITE:
At the first sign of trouble, the multinational team swings into action. Here Capt. Robert Benson radios preliminary findings during a rescue exercise. Dutch MPs and a U.S. medical unit stand by to assist.

Critical seconds tick by as Chief Air Staff Officer Major Charlie Haydar awaits news of an UNTSO flight that has apparently gone astray. Due to regional disputes, what should be an 18-minute flight from Jerusalem to Amman actually takes over two hours, travelling a circuitous path through international airspace.

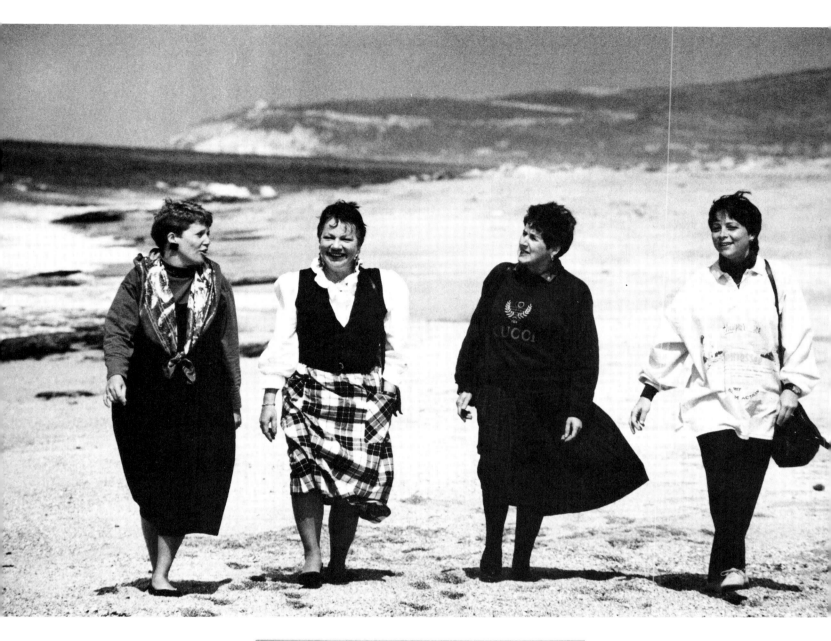

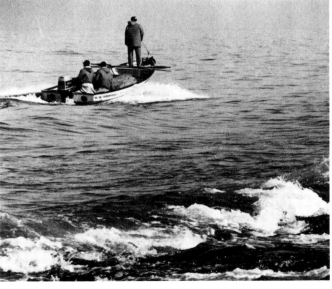

Walking the beach at Nahariya, the wives of Canadian observers with UNTSO compare experiences. (*Left to right:* Nancy Follwell, Donna Smith, Toni Porter, Lucie Leblanc.)

Calm seas – for the present – greet a fishing boat chugging out of the ancient harbour at Akko in northern Israel. This part of the Mediterranean has in past years been the scene of dramatic amphibious strikes and counterstrikes by Israeli and Palestinian commando units.

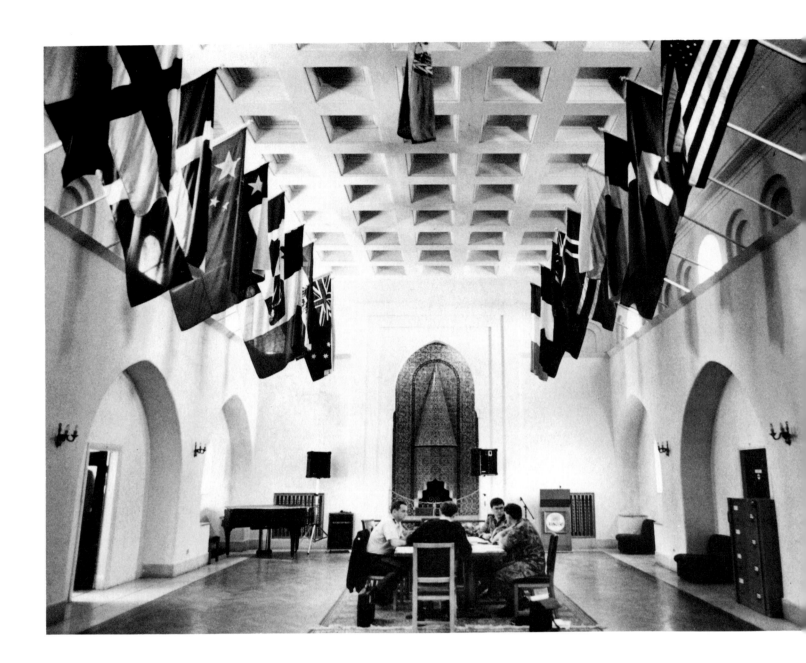

The staff room in UNTSO headquarters displays flags of all 19 nations participating under the UN banner. "It's really a mini–United Nations," says Maj. Charlie Haydar. "The skills they bring are skills common to all the military services of all the countries that contribute to the UN."

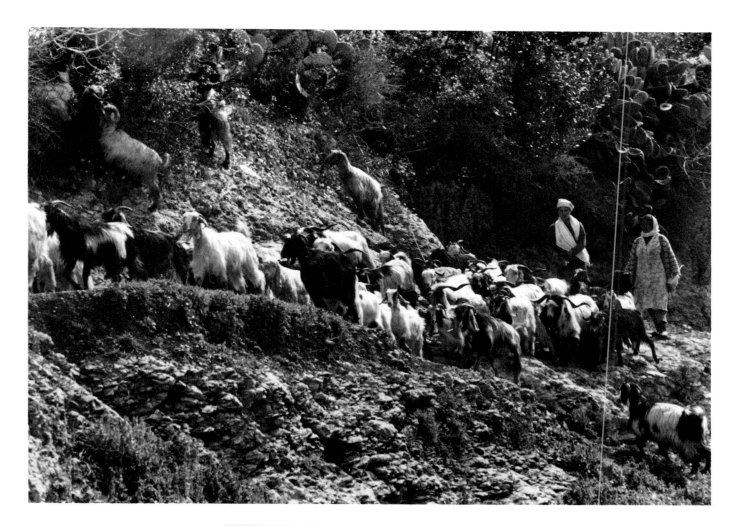

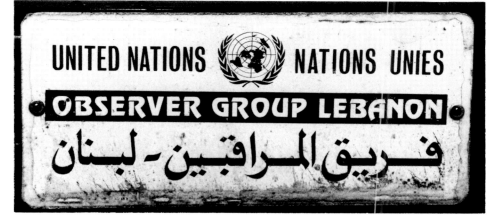

The rocky hills of southern Lebanon offer meagre grazing for shepherds driving their goats to greener pastures. "The Lebanese people are an enduring lot," says Capt. Jim Follwell. "Some days must look hopeless to them. But there is that ray of light – the UN presence – that tells them one day there's going to be something better."

"You never drive alone," says Maj. Paul Andrews. "You don't want to be mistaken for a terrorist and shot on sight. The UN emblem is always displayed, the flag is up, and for night driving (which requires special permission) the dome light is on and so is the flag light. You proceed very, very cautiously."

Uncharacteristically sombre, children in embattled Alma Ech-Chaab await a funeral procession. "Observer Group Lebanon is fairly popular," says Capt. Jim Follwell. "You get little kids waving, and most people smile. It's when they stop that you can tell something's going wrong."

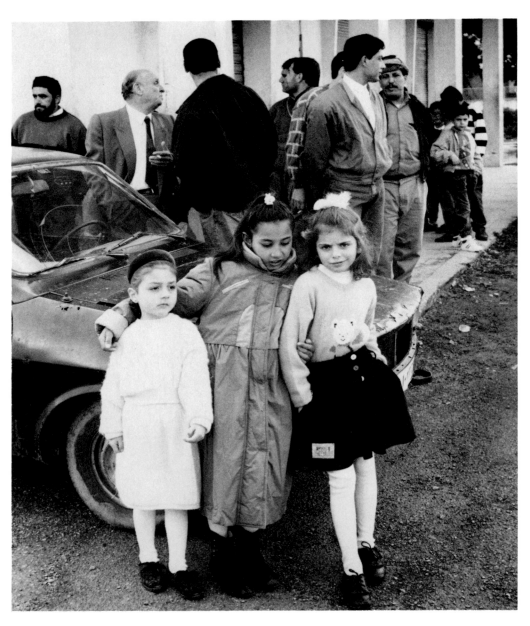

Lt.-Col. Bill Porter visits Alma-Ech Chaab in southern Lebanon for a word with the town's mayor. "Flying the flag" – showing a UN presence – is a vital though risky part of UNTSO mobile patrol.

Flak jackets are required equipment. Although UN people are not usually targeted directly, artillery and car bombs intended for other groups present serious threats.

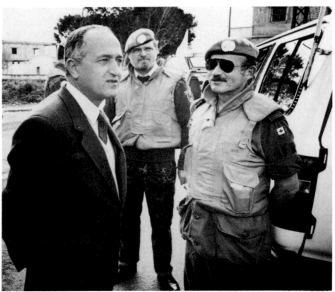

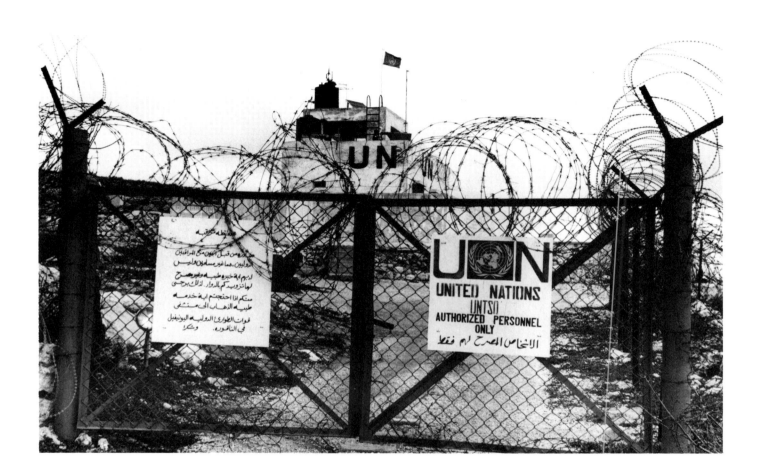

The difficulties faced by Canadian observers in southern Lebanon include the occasional tedium of the job itself. "You have days of looking at nothing but a fence," says UNTSO's Capt. Jim Follwell.

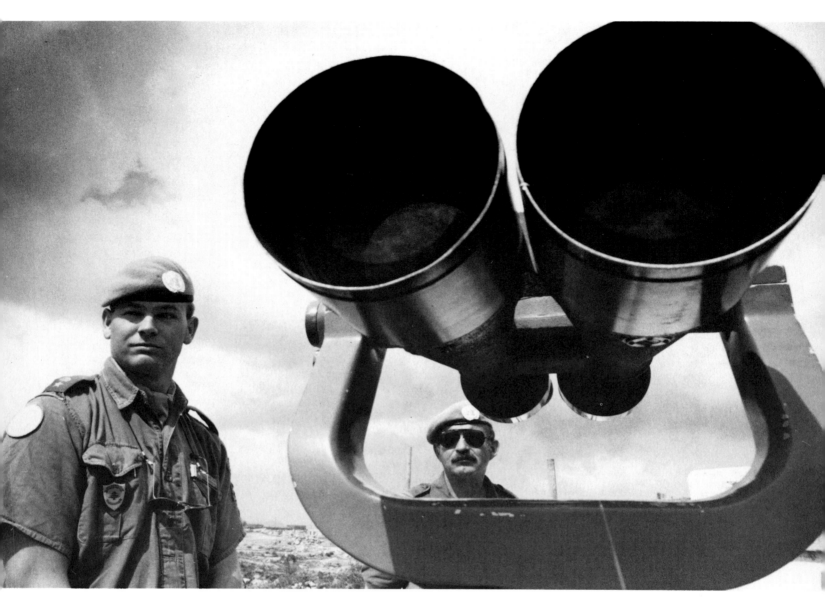

ABOVE:

By scanning the horizon from the OP HIN lookout, Lt. Col. Bill Porter, commander of UNTSO Observer Group Lebanon (*right*), and a Swedish major keep a close watch for ceasefire infractions.

"Being out on an observation post is, for the bulk of the time, quite dull," says UNTSO Capt. Dan Leblanc (*far right*). "There are long stretches of utter boredom, interrupted now and then by periods of high excitement."

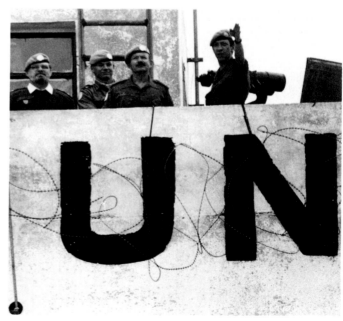

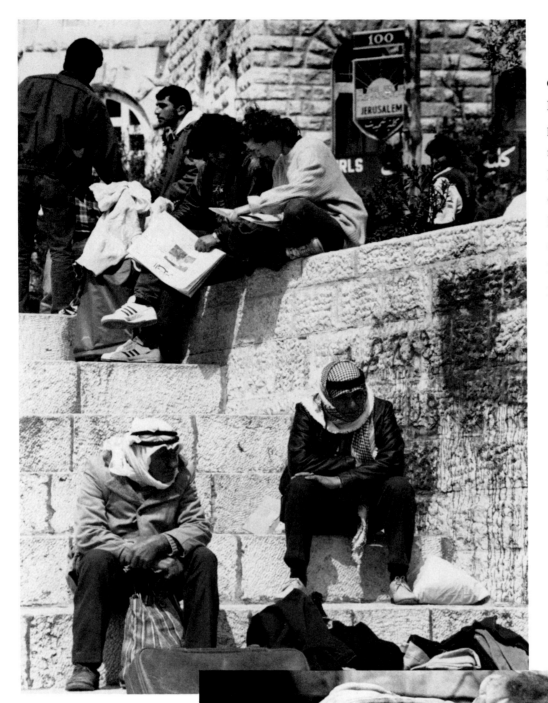

OPPOSITE:
Emigrating to the promised land confers mixed blessings for Russian Jews like this cellist in Tel Aviv. Free at last from Soviet intolerance, they dream now of lasting harmony between Israel and its Palestinian neighbours.

Though miles apart ideologically, Arabs and Jews rub shoulders in the Old City of Jerusalem's congested passages.

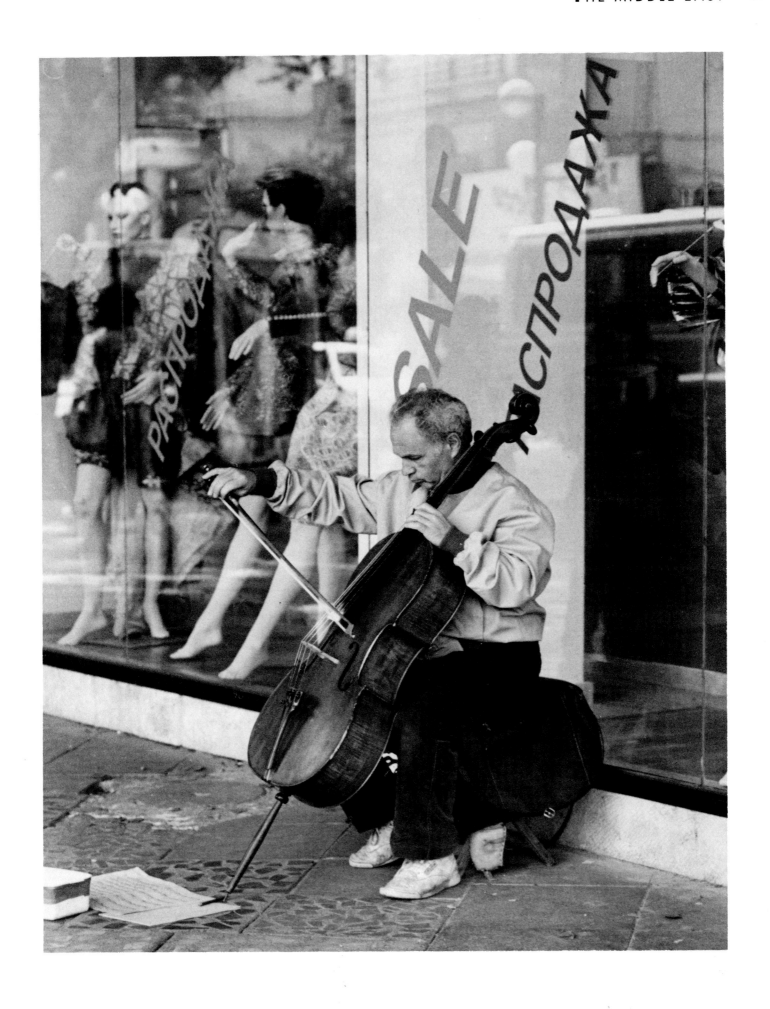

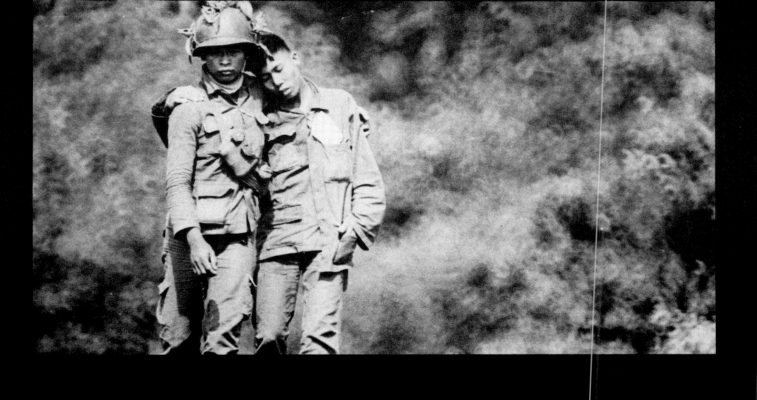

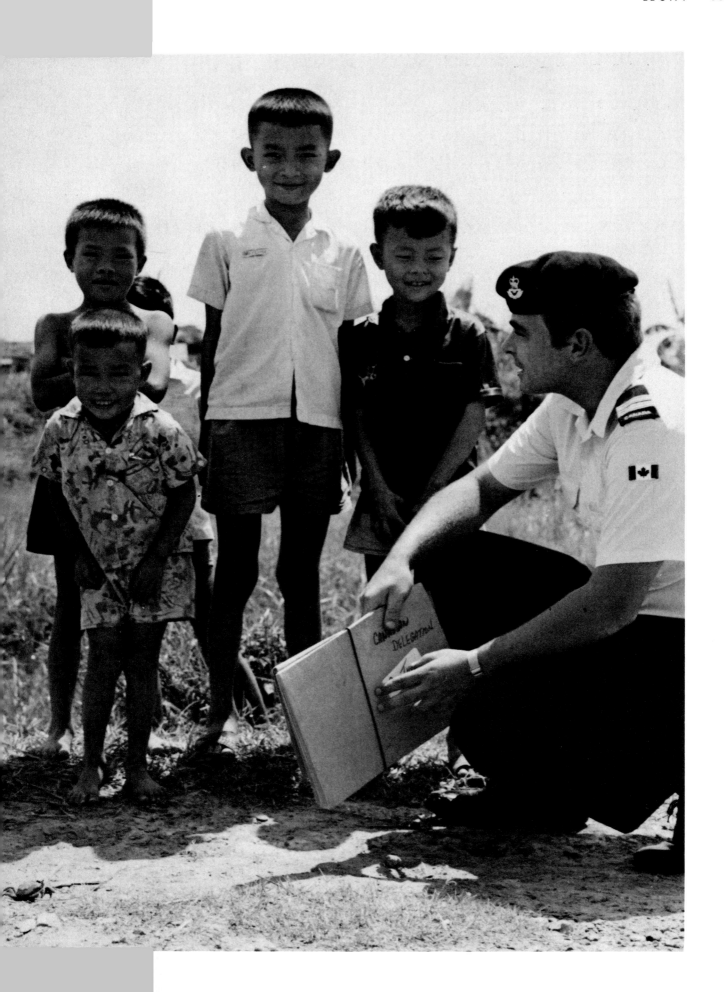

PAGE 82:

Walking wounded. A
South Vietnamese trooper
(in camouflaged helmet)
helps an injured comrade
to an aid station following
a clash between govern-
ment troops and North
Vietnamese forces in
1974. Frustrated by two
decades of ultimately
unsuccessful efforts at
peacekeeping in Vietnam,
Canada had withdrawn
the previous year.

PREVIOUS PAGE:

Making friends with
local children is a small
but simple investment
towards future peace –
and perhaps it makes
home and family seem
a little less far away.
Vietnam, 1973.

HISTORICALLY, CANADIANS HAVE LOOKED across the
Atlantic rather than the Pacific. Our great wars have been mainly in Europe, as
well as our military alliances. The Korean War, a stalemated struggle that is
neglected in our history books, has failed to make much of a mark on our collective consciousness.

This is also true of Canada's peacekeeping efforts in Asia. They receive
nothing like the attention won by Pearson's Nobel Peace Prize, the three-decade-
long experience in Cyprus, or the more recent operations in the Persian Gulf. And
yet Canada has been involved in five Asian peacekeeping forces: two along the
troubled borders between India, Pakistan, and Afghanistan, and three in the
nations that sprang into existence from French Indo-China.

The UN's second peacekeeping operation was in the disputed princely states
of Jammu and Kashmir, areas left over after the partition of British India into the
republics of India and Pakistan in 1948. With Hindu rulers and predominantly
Muslim populations, Jammu and Kashmir were almost bound to be subjects of
conflict. The trouble escalated from clashes between irregular bands to full-
blown battles between the regular Indian and Pakistani armies. In December 1948
the United Nations asked for military observers to be sent to help keep the peace,
and in February Canada quietly and without publicity responded by sending four
army officers. Significantly, Ottawa dispatched reserve force officers; by 1949 the
regular army was deemed too short of officers to spare any. Several months later
an additional four officers were sent to Kashmir with equal discretion – perhaps
this dispute between two Commonwealth nations was considered unseemly by the
Department of External Affairs.

The observers serving with the United Nations Military Observer Group in
India and Pakistan (UNMOGIP) operated at extraordinarily high altitudes (above
5,000 metres in some cases) and in difficult terrain. They investigated com-

A Canadian Caribou
delivers a UN jeep to
military observers with
UNMOGIP in Kargil,
India. The Kargil air strip
is almost 3,000 metres
above sea level, deep in
the Himalaya range.

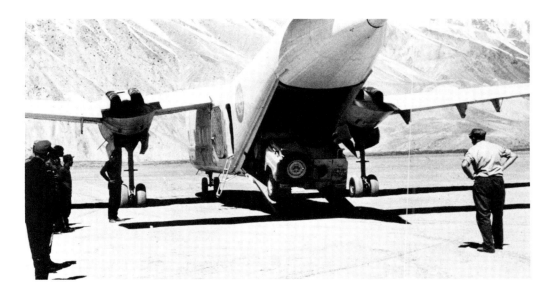

plaints, kept track of the arms and equipment on both sides, and tried to avoid boredom. But ennui could disappear quickly when tension between India and Pakistan increased, as it did after 1963. Canada agreed then to increase its observer contribution to nine (of a total of forty) and to provide a Caribou aircraft and crew. The aircraft, but happily not the crew, became the first casualty of the war between India and Pakistan in September 1965, when it was destroyed on the ground by Pakistani forces.

Kashmir was only one of the locales of action during the brief war, and UNMOGIP was powerless to stop such full-scale combat. Nonetheless, the force was strengthened with thirty more observers, including ten more Canadians, and the Security Council established a new force, the United Nations India–Pakistan Observation Mission. UNIPOM was charged with supervising the ceasefire and the withdrawal of forces in all areas other than Kashmir, and a Canadian, Major-General Bruce Macdonald, who had been serving in Cyprus, took command of its hundred observers. Canada provided twelve observers and five aircraft and their air and ground crews.

UNIPOM was a success and the status quo was restored. The force withdrew in March 1966. But UNMOGIP continues in place to the present, though since 1979 Canada has provided only periodic airlift support to it.

Canada's latest peacekeeping role on the subcontinent took place in 1988, when the long guerrilla war against the Communist regime in Afghanistan began to draw to a close. The Soviet Union, clearly beginning to unravel, agreed to withdraw its military forces from the country, while the United States undertook to stop its support for the rebels. The Afghanis, in effect, would be left to fight it out on their own. But the process required supervision and the UN formed the United Nations Good Offices Mission in Afghanistan and Pakistan (UNGOMAP) to assist. A handful of Canadians participated as observers. More significantly,

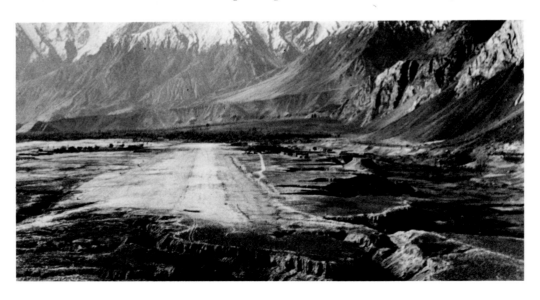

The Skardu runway – despite the fissures in the foreground, one of the better mountain landing-strips in Pakistan. Canadian crews serving with UNMOGIP transported observers, mail, and supplies to many such air strips along the ceasefire line.

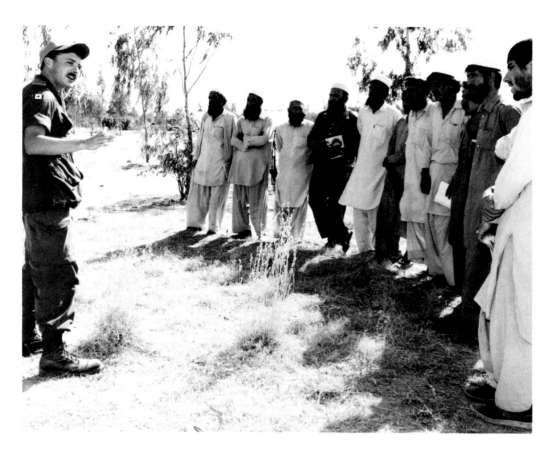

A lesson in survival draws the full attention of Afghan refugees as a Canadian sergeant covers the basics of mine recognition. Fifty Canadian military engineers participated in the UN-sponsored program, offering mine awareness training to more than 150,000 Afghans.

A simple story with a life-or-death message, this silkscreen illustrates an everyday event for returning Afghans. *From right to left*: a butterfly mine, a boy spots it, he tells an adult, the adult marks it, and they both tell a "deminer" trained through the UN program to disarm and destroy mines. These cloth silkscreens could be used to make household items like clothing, bags, and tablecloths. Ideally they would stay in the home with the student, reinforcing the lessons of the program.

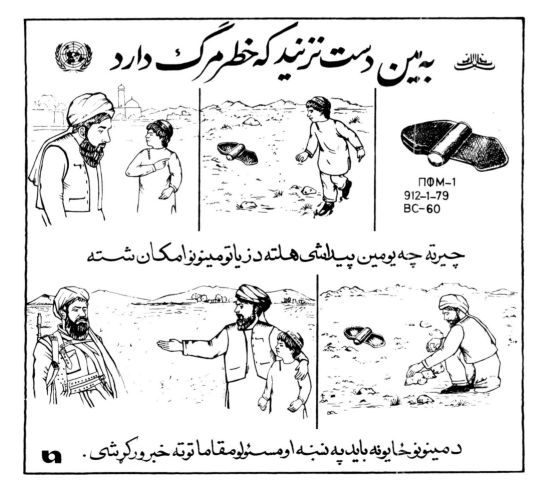

because the Pakistan–Afghanistan border had been sown with mines and booby-traps and women and children were dying as a result, Canada agreed to contribute to the Mine Awareness Clearance Training Program. Thirteen mine warfare experts, including female soldiers, lectured in refugee camps on the Pakistani side of the border, providing demonstrations of what to avoid and how to disarm mines that could not be avoided.

The situation in Indo-China was even more complex. The French had reoccupied their colonies after the end of the Second World War, and had quickly fallen into a struggle against the forces of Vietnamese nationalism. Exhausted by 1954, France threw up its hands and turned the fate of the area over to a Great Power meeting in Geneva. The result was a decision to create three new nations, Laos, Cambodia, and Vietnam. The last of these was to be divided between a Communist north and a non-Communist south until free elections could determine the popular will.

To supervise the withdrawal of forces and the movements of refugees, the Great Powers established a three-nation International Commission for Supervision and Control. (Its three teams – for the three troubled nations – were always known as the International Control Commissions, or ICCs.) The members of each troika, the powers declared, were to be from Communist Poland, neutral India, and democratic Canada – though none of the countries had been asked in advance.

Canada sent three ambassadors to head its teams, diplomats and the requisite staffs, and eighty-three officers, including three major-generals, along with thirty-one other ranks. Almost all the officers were bilingual, a virtual necessity in the French-speaking area, and this caused a serious strain on the military's resources at home. The first Canadians arrived by August 1954.

In Laos and Cambodia, the ICCs' work was handled with relative dispatch and wound down fairly quickly (though a flare-up in Laos led to the commission's

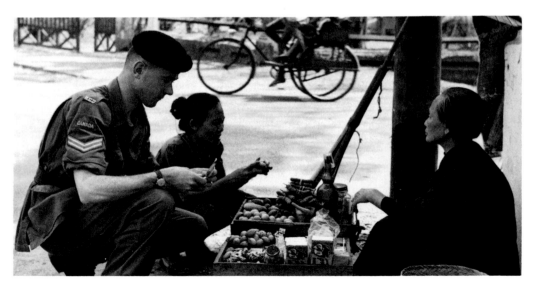

Canadians served on the ICSC in Laos from 1954 to 1969, alongside contingents from India and Poland. Although the "troika" of observing nations was often less a balance than a tug-of-war, the intervention was relatively successful.

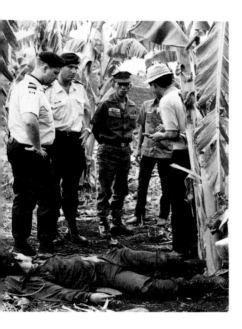

In Vietnam the ICSC made no headway, and its successor, the ICCS, could only monitor the war that ensued. This team views the body of a Viet Cong fighter killed in a battle with the South Vietnamese Army in 1973.

re-establishment in 1961). But in Vietnam, a casualty of the Cold War, the task was difficult indeed. Some 700,000 refugees were moved promptly to the north or south, the armed forces were concentrated, and 75,000 prisoners were exchanged, but then a long guerrilla war began over the future of the region. The Viet Minh, the government in the north, sponsored the Viet Cong, a nationalist and Communist guerrilla movement in the south. The south, emboldened by the support of the United States, refused to agree to elections, and the ICC found its work frustrated.

Although the Canadians had intended to be impartial, they found that the Poles were always partisan in their judgements on complaints, while the Indians wavered uneasily back and forth. Complicating matters further, once the United States began to participate heavily in the Vietnam War in the early 1960s, were the ties of friendship and alliance that bound Canada and the U.S. Many Canadian officers had served with American forces; most, after seeing the effects of Communist subversion in Vietnam, sympathized with them; and there were strong pressures, frequently not overcome, to share intelligence and information. The ICC in effect became a victim of the war, its Canadian observers filing complaints against Communist violations while the Poles denied their existence; the Poles pointing to every instance of American involvement or southern violation of the Geneva Accords while the Canadians almost always discounted them. Not until the Paris peace agreement of January 1973 nominally brought the war to a close was the ICC allowed to wind up its by-now farcical role.

But the end of the Vietnam ICC was followed by the establishment of the new International Commission for Control and Supervision (ICCS), a reborn four-nation ICC. Once more Canada found itself pulled (this time kicking and screaming) into Vietnam, its partners in this round being Communist Hungary and

Members of the ICCS and the Joint Military Command hold an open-air conference to discuss a POW exchange at Loc Ninh, 160 km from Saigon, in 1973.

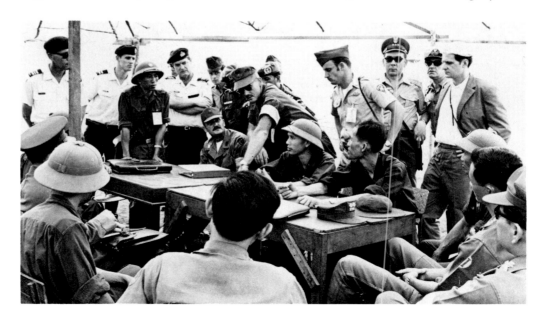

Poland and "democratic" Indonesia.

Forced to participate by American insistence, Ottawa decided that this time matters would be handled differently. Instead of suffering in silence, Canadian members of the new ICCS would follow an "open mouth" policy of publicly pointing out truce violations on either side, and making it clear to all whenever the Poles and Hungarians were obstructing the commission's work. Moreover, Canada agreed to contribute its team of 50 External Affairs officers and 230 service personnel for only a two-month period. The observer teams took the field quickly to monitor the inflow of war material and the exchange of prisoners of war.

But almost at once the old ICC pattern reasserted itself, as the Poles and Hungarians again turned a blind eye to Communist violations. Canadian protests were loud but largely unavailing, and Ottawa gave notice of its intention to depart. American pleas led to a four-month extension, but Canada withdrew from the ICCS at the end of July 1973. One Canadian officer had been killed when North Vietnamese troops shot down his helicopter; other Canadians had been captured and held by the Viet Cong, but fortunately later released. The Canadian experience in Vietnam, two decades long, was completely frustrating.

Perhaps that explains Canada's reluctance to commit large numbers to the United Nations Transitional Authority in Cambodia, an immense peacekeeping operation created in the early months of 1992. Projected to have 22,000 members and to cost more than $2 billion, UNTAC was assigned the task of running Cambodia while its factions sorted themselves out, the guerrilla war (with luck) ceased, and refugees were resettled. Canada agreed to provide 200 specialists for the operation, a creditable contribution but a very small one. The experience in the successor states of French Indo-China had been so negative, so futile, that Ottawa's lack of enthusiasm was eminently understandable.

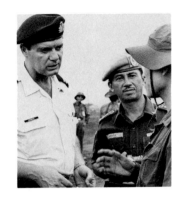

Canadian officers chatting with a Viet Cong soldier at a POW exchange (*above*), and keeping an eye on Viet Cong prisoners changing out of prison garb (*below left*), in 1973. Monitoring the "cease-fire" and supervising exchanges of POWs and detainees were the ICCS's main tasks.

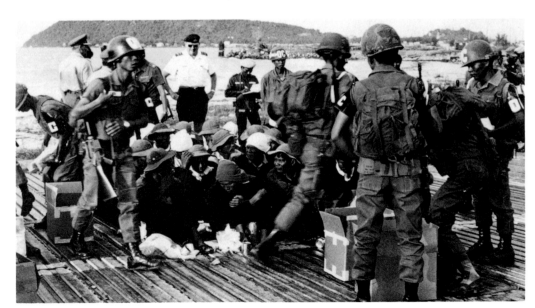

GROUNDFIRE PORT SIDE

MAJOR PAT DILLON
Vietnam

The "conflict" in Vietnam was a war that never stopped in all the time we were there. It was never a ceasefire. It was just a less-fire. And it depended on where you were how *much* of a less-fire it was.

I ended up commanding a teamsite in Vi Thanh, on the lower Mekong Delta. Our job was investigating incidents, and checking the flow of troops and equipment down the Ho Chi Minh Trail.

One morning we were flying back from Tri Tôn, on the Cambodian border, when we hit heavy cloud. Our normal flight plan called for a minimum 3,000-metre altitude, high enough to avoid becoming somebody's target. But this was monsoon season and the only way of getting home was to fly underneath the clouds.

Six weeks before this I had seen our escort helicopter shot down before my eyes, so by now I had a

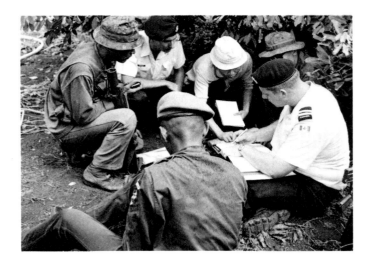

Lone witness to a 1973 Viet Cong ambush, a South Vietnamese soldier tells two ICCS officers about the attack that killed the rest of his patrol. "It was never a ceasefire," recalls Major Pat Dillon. "It was just a less-fire. And it depended on where you were how *much* of a less-fire it was."

fairly high twitch factor. We were flying along a series of canals just north-west of Vi Thanh. I was wearing an armoured helmet, sitting on a flak jacket, and wearing another one. My wife had given me strict instructions about taking certain precautions.

I was sitting with my feet in the gunner's sling. There was no gun, but they put the sling in the door to keep you cool as you were flying along. Looking down, I saw a person run out of the bush. He picked something up, pointed it at us, and the next thing I knew we had rounds all around the helicopter. As the rounds passed they sounded just like popping corn.

The crew chief got on the radio and put out a "groundfire port side" report. I sent a Mayday and a grid reference. Suddenly the aircraft kicked up. We'd received a couple of rounds in the rear. The helicopter went into a screaming dive. It was hairy as hell. It was the first time I had ever gone straight down in a helicopter. If you really want to get an adrenalin high first thing in the morning, I can recommend that.

The guys who flew those things were fantastic. They were all Air America pilots with three or four thousand hours on those aircraft. They could put them into manoeuvres you wouldn't think possible. The pilot pulled out at the last second and we made a rather interesting bump on the ground.

We got out and had a look, but there were other people down there. This was right in the middle of Indian country. They knew they didn't have any helicopters; so as far as they were concerned it didn't matter how we were painted – everybody was enemy. The engine was still running and we decided quickly to take off again.

We flew the rest of the way to Vi Thanh right on the deck. I'd always enjoyed flying in helicopters before. It was never the same afterwards.

Major Dillon served with the International Commission for Control and Supervision in 1973.

DIARY FROM AN LOC

CAPTAIN MIKE DION

Vietnam

AN LOC. APRIL 5, 1973 As we look down on our compound from the helicopter, the realities of the Vietnam War sink in. The aerial view is like something out of a nightmare scene, devoid of life and colour. The rubber trees are nothing more than gaunt grey sentinels – mute reminders of a division-sized battle – as the triple rows of truck-sized craters are reminders of the B-52s. Our tiny compound is but an island in this sea of dead, burned sticks rising out of the omnipresent red dust.

APRIL 8 We just learned that an ICCS helicopter was shot down yesterday, killing all aboard including [Canadian] Captain Charlie Laviolette. As a result, all ICCS helicopters have been grounded. We are cut off from Saigon.

APRIL 14 Our camp guards shot a bamboo viper today. It is better known as a "two-step", because you only have time to take two steps after being bitten.

Our stock of food is now reduced to macaroni and fried oatmeal. ICCS flights are still grounded. However, the South Vietnamese agree to resupply us.

MAY 9 Sporadic fighting has broken out four kilometres south-west of us and ten kilometres to the north. Strike aircraft pass close overhead. One A-1 Skyraider circles overhead with a bomb dangling from one wing. The bomb breaks loose and explodes harmlessly in the jungle.

MAY 23 Two ICCS helicopters pass over to make an investigation thirty kilometres north of us. As soon as they fly south again, the fighting resumes.

JUNE 8 A regimental-strength attack is going on three kilometres to the south-west of us. The position six hundred metres west of us fired two hundred artillery rounds yesterday. Today the count is five hundred. Some of the rounds pass right over our heads. We see the low-elevation rounds, and get a little nervous.

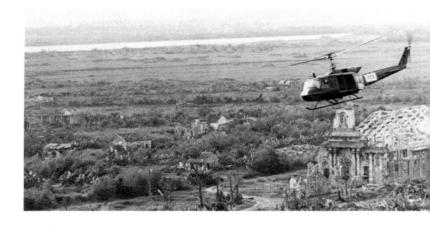

An ICCS helicopter flies over the devastated Vietnamese city of Quang Tri in March 1973. One Canadian peacekeeper was killed when his helicopter was shot down by Viet Cong.

JUNE 9 The situation has become so serious that two helicopters have been placed on thirty minutes' notice to move should evacuation of our site become necessary.

JUNE 12 The fighting in the south-west has died down. However, five 122mm rockets land on the southern edge of An Loc. These weapons have a tremendous penetrating capability, but they're woefully inaccurate when fired from *ad hoc* bamboo launchers. We are now wearing flak jackets, even at night.

JUNE 17 The fighting has died down. An ICCS flight is expected shortly, and we are to leave on it. On the way in, the two helicopters come under fire. No one is hurt, and the aircraft arrive unscathed except for a bullet hole in one rotor blade. After ten weeks of negotiations for guarantees of safety, the helicopters are still targets.

For the return flight we fly at 3,000 metres, out of range of local weapons. The ICCS site at An Loc is closed.

Captain Dion was a member of the International Commission for Control and Supervision in Vietnam in 1973; his mission lasted just seventy-five days. Excerpts from his diary appeared in the Canadian Forces magazine Sentinel, *1978/1.*

EIGHTEEN DAYS AT DUC CO

MAJOR JOCK ROSS

Vietnam

On March 1, 1973, two fully loaded helicopters stood beside the Region Three Headquarters in Pleiku. The atmosphere was tense as we speculated on whether it would be a "go" or "no go" for our first teamsite in PRG – Provisional Revolutionary Government – country at Duc Co.

The phone rang; it was Saigon. The conversation was short. "OK, let's go!"

We were airborne at 1,500 metres within minutes – too high to be hit by small-arms fire. The flight from Pleiku to Duc Co, near the Cambodian border, took twenty minutes. A helicopter flight was the only way in and, more important to us, the only way out.

Adhering to a tight traffic pattern, we descended towards the two crosses between the dove-of-peace flags. The two aircraft set down and shut down. Not a soul was in sight.

The feeling was eerie. We knew we were under observation. It was so quiet we could almost hear the flowers eating the insects (which they did). The next day we discovered that we had been in the sights of Viet Cong guns situated only thirty metres away.

Suffocating heat reflected up from the metal mattress airstrip. Strange insects squeaked and chirped amid the mangled war hardware scattered everywhere. Live grenades, bombs, rockets, and shells lined the runway.

After five interminable minutes, pith helmets rose over the horizon, then shoulders, then waists. We exchanged big smiles. Our PRG hosts greeted us with bone-crushing handshakes.

In early March we became aware that a small war was going on about twenty-five kilometres north-east of us, on the route to Pleiku. The U.S. Air Force was supporting the Army of the Republic of Vietnam, and

from our position we could watch the B-52s fly in three at a time, high, in line-astern formation. Then we'd watch for the telltale turn as they formed up side by side for their bomb run. From a distance the mattress bombing sounded like a nervous person tapping ten fingers on a wooden table.

Each day the battle intensified and moved closer. By March 12 we were pressed by the other ICCS members to agree to a unanimous request for evacuation. Our Viet Cong hosts allocated bunkers to us, and we did a little personal administration in case all did not go well. But we decided to stay.

On the evening of March 15, the Hungarian delegate with us became so sick he couldn't walk. At 2200 hours I was surprised when out of the bushes walked a ghost all dressed in white, wearing a stethoscope around its neck. It was the Viet Cong doctor. He took a blood sample and diagnosed malaria right on the spot, using equipment he carried in his pocket.

My turn to get sick came on March 18, and I was medically evacuated, as was the remainder of the ICCS team, just two months after it arrived at Duc Co.

Duc Co was one of thirty-five International Commission for Control and Supervision teamsites in Vietnam where Canadian observers served. In this account, published in the Sentinel, 1978/1, *Major Ross also noted that the Duc Co site was obliterated after his departure, when fifty-eight air strikes were directed against its fifteen rickety structures.*

DEATH OF A TWIN OTTER

LIEUTENANT-COLONEL SYD BURROWS

India–Pakistan

In 1971, I picked up a brand-new Twin Otter from de Havilland in Toronto, painted white with the blue United Nations symbols and lettering. As a member of the peacekeeping mission to India–Pakistan, I was to fly the aircraft to Kashmir to replace one of our older Caribous.

Captain Bob Jenkinson, crewman Master Corporal Dan Hornik, and I took off from Trenton on a route that would take us via Frobisher, Søndre Strømfjord, Keflavík, London, Lahr, Rome, Athens, Beirut, Bahrain, Karachi, Chaklala, and Srinagar – sixty-five hours' flying time, and halfway around the world.

Flying in the Himalayas was awe-inspiring. They are breathtaking mountains, and the Twin Otter was ideal for the high-altitude Himalayan conditions. Our duties involved transporting UN military observers, mail, and supplies to the many small, difficult, and interesting airstrips along the ceasefire line. We operated out of the main airfield at Srinagar during the summer months, and out of Chaklala, the international airport at Rawalpindi, Pakistan, during the winter months.

On December 3 a war broke out between West Pakistan and India. The air war raged over us, the airfield, and our vulnerable Twin Otter. In an effort to establish a ceasefire, our chief military observer, a Chilean lieutenant-general, advised me to prepare the Twin Otter for a flight through the war zone from Chaklala to New Delhi.

We waited all of the next day, through several strafing attacks by Indian Air Force fighters, for clearance to fly. Because the fighters ignored our UN Twin Otter, we assumed they had decided to leave us alone.

Early the following morning they returned. Firing 30mm high-explosive cannon shells, they strafed and blew our lovely flying machine to hell. I later heard, but could never confirm, the reason they hit us on the ground. It meant they could then shoot down any Pakistan International Airlines Twin Otters, which were painted white like ours, without the risk of downing UN peacekeepers.

Lieutenant-Colonel Burrows's detachment was airlifted back to Canada, and then returned with another Twin Otter roughly a month later. He completed his tour with the UN Military Observer Group in India and Pakistan in 1972.

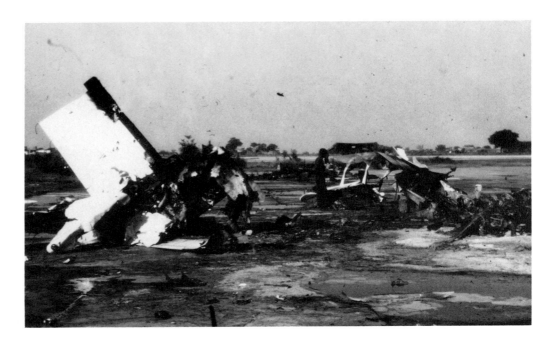

The runway in Rawalpindi, Pakistan, strewn with the wreckage of Lt.-Col. Burrows's Twin Otter, after the Indian Air Force "blew our lovely flying machine to hell."

THE KABUL GOLF AND COUNTRY CLUB

MAJOR GEORDIE ELMS
Pakistan–Afghanistan

In the spring of 1989, on three days' notice, I found myself with four other officers at an Ottawa briefing for the first new UN peacekeeping mission in nearly a decade. Rather than observing a ceasefire, we would be monitoring a political agreement between Afghanistan and Pakistan. The Afghan resistance, the Mujahideen, was not party to the accord and had not agreed to stop fighting.

We landed in Islamabad, Pakistan. A few days later, Lieutenant-Colonel Dave Leslie and Major Pat Chartres became the first Canadian officials to arrive in Afghanistan in eight years. Five months later, halfway through the Soviet withdrawal, they returned from Kabul to duty at the Islamabad Station, and Captain Murray Allan and I took their places.

In Kabul we joined a small group, fewer than forty, composed of officers drawn from ten countries, with members of the UN Field Service drawn from at least ten more. It was a new mission, and there were many frustrations. We all worked to make the best of things, whether it be starting the generator, which gave us light and communications, or hauling sandbags for shelters to protect us from flying debris and shrapnel.

One of my duties took me to the world's coldest Observation Post, at Hayratan, on the River Amu Darya, which separated Afghanistan from the U.S.S.R. Over six weeks, I watched and counted with a team of officers from Nepal, Denmark, and Ghana, as nearly 40,000 Soviets left for home.

There was little to do in terms of recreation, even in the city of Kabul. A government-imposed curfew had pretty much shut down the activities of the few international community clubs. One activity some of us enjoyed was membership in the world's most exclusive club, the Kabul Golf and Country Club. Every Friday morning, weather permitting – and if there wasn't a

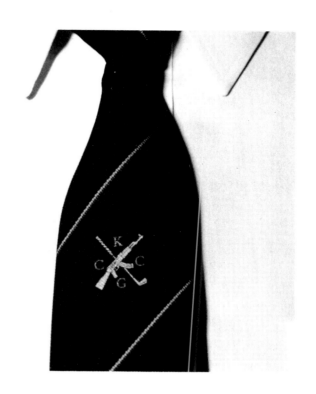

A golf iron crossed with an assault rifle adorns the tie of the world's most "exclusive" club, the Kabul Golf and Country Club.

Soviet battalion parked on the fairways – a small band of stalwarts made their way to the Kharg Lake area west of the city.

The clubhouse still stood – or at least most of the walls – but we did have to supply our own nineteenth-hole facilities. The fairways were rocky, and greens were fashioned from brown sand, but still it was fun. Sometimes we could hear the sound of outgoing rounds passing overhead, as the Soviets and Afghans fired into the hills beyond the outer perimeter of defences which ringed the city.

Having played the course and paid the requisite fees, a member was entitled to purchase the club tie, suitably adorned with its crest – a golf club crossed with an AK assault rifle. Only two Canadians, Major Chartres and I, have the rare privilege of wearing it.

Major Elms was assigned to the UN Good Offices Mission in Afghanistan and Pakistan.

MINES DON'T TAKE SIDES

CAPTAIN JANE THELWELL

Pakistan

I was with the first group of Canadians in Peshawar, teaching mine safety to Afghan refugees. There were actually two programs – mine awareness for the Afghan women and children, and mine clearance for the men.

We passed the word about the dangers of the mines in any way we could. Often we'd arrange to visit a refugee camp; once there, we'd be invited into one of the more liberal households. Soon neighbours would start showing up, along with twenty or thirty children, and it could get to be quite a zoo.

It was a very dynamic learning environment. You couldn't lecture at them. You had to tell stories, and let them tell you stories in return. For instance, I'd pick up a butterfly mine, and somebody would go into a long story about old Uncle Abdul who had picked one up, and how he had lost his fingers. "Oh, and by the way," they'd tell everyone, "Uncle Abdul's camels are dead now. . . ." And so on. Twenty minutes later we'd get back to the class. At first it seemed very slow, coming from our structured learning environments. But that's the way it had to be done.

We'd take dummy mines with us, or mines with the explosives removed. We also had posters showing the various mines people might encounter. One day we held up one of the anti-tank mines and asked whether anyone knew what it was. One lady put up her hand and in genuine earnest said, "It's for cooking. It's a pot." Well, no wonder these people were dying when they went back to Afghanistan. Very few women would actually recognize a mine if they saw one.

Sometimes we would even set up little minefields inside one of their enclosed yards. We'd have them walk around to see if they could identify mines and ordnance. It was amazing; when you put trip wires on the mines, most of the women would walk right over them. They had to get attuned to looking for those things.

Another point we tried to make was that it didn't matter where the mines had come from. Mines left by Afghan rebels were as much a threat as those placed by the Soviets. If you stepped on one, it could still kill you. They had to keep their eyes open at all times. Mines don't take sides.

In 1989 Captain Thelwell taught mine safety to Afghan refugees near the Pakistan border as part of a UN humanitarian assistance program.

Gingerly prodding for the telltale feel of a buried land mine, Afghans at a refugee camp on the Pakistan border learn new life skills under the watchful eye of Canadian Forces instructors. An estimated 30 million mines still litter Afghan- istan – roughly two for each of the country's 15 million people.

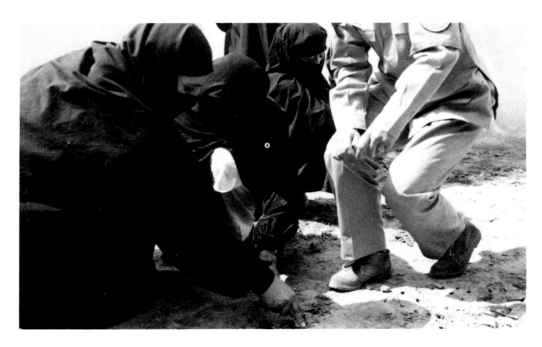

THE FEELING OF FREEDOM

CAPTAIN SYLVIE LEMIEUX
Pakistan

I'm very independent. I love the freedom to act more or less as I choose. That's one thing I missed in Pakistan. There, a woman cannot safely walk alone. But on any peacekeeping or humanitarian mission you have to adjust to the culture. You have to accommodate the customs of the people you are trying to help.

In the refugee camps, that meant wearing a veil. I found that hard. Because the men, not the women, said I had to wear one, I had no choice. I had to abide by their rules. I found it particularly tough putting that veil over my head.

Another thing we learned was not to look at people directly, especially men. Not to look into their eyes. And not to shake anyone's hand. Instead, you'd put your right hand over your chest and bend slightly. That was their way of greeting. Holding out your hand was a sign of rudeness.

We were often invited into people's homes. If somebody offered you something, like food or tea, it was always best to refuse the first time: "Oh, no, thank you. You go to too much trouble. . . ." Then they would offer again, and if you were watching your manners you would decline a second time: "No, really, I'm fine. You're so kind. I don't want to put you to any trouble. . . ." Only on the third request was it polite to accept.

You even had to watch the way you sat down on a carpet. You had to take great care where you pointed your toes. In Canada we're used to sitting on chairs with our feet out in front of us. Over there, when you remove your shoes and sit on a carpet, it is most improper to point your feet in anyone's direction. You tuck them under your bum. That's not easy. Sitting on your legs gets very uncomfortable. We'd often stay at one place for several hours. After a while you'd feel like you just had to get up and walk around, but proper etiquette required you to keep still.

Despite our sometimes great ignorance, we were very well received. In that culture, the women and kids are the ones who fetch the wood and clear the land for planting. They would be continually coming into contact

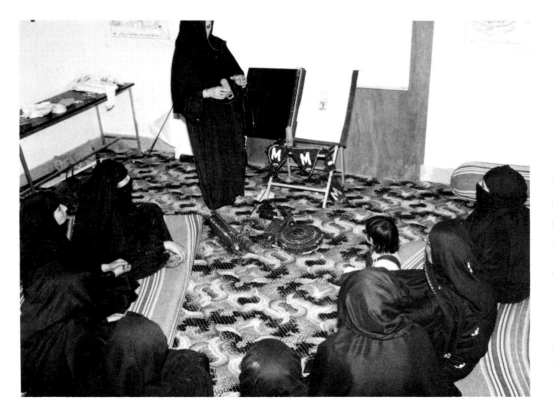

A variety of disabled mines at the feet of a Canadian-taught master trainer help illustrate the dangers of unexploded ordnance. Muslim strictures permitted only *female* mine experts to present sessions to refugee women and children.

with unexploded mines and mortar shells left over from the war in Afghanistan. The more you learned about the way they lived, the more you realized how important our job was.

It was a great experience, a great opportunity. But when I got home, the first thing I did was to go for a walk. By myself. It was so good, getting back that feeling of freedom.

Captain Lemieux took part, in 1990, in the UN humanitarian assistance program for displaced Afghans along the Pakistan border.

REVERSE CULTURE SHOCK

CAPTAIN DEBORAH WOLFE
Pakistan

A lot of the refugees in the Afghan camps were either widows or women separated from their husbands during the fighting. Conservative Muslim tradition forbids women of that culture from being seen or spoken to by any male other than men related to them. Even their hair has to be covered when they are outside the home. Yet these women were expected to return to Afghanistan, with their children, through territory littered with land mines. That's why we were there with Operation Salaam. There were two female Canadian officers in my group, Captain Sylvie Lemieux and me, teaching refugee women mine awareness. Otherwise, there was no way they were all going to make it home in one piece.

We worked mainly preparing master trainers, well-educated Afghan women who could go to the various camps and spread the word about the dangers of mines and unexploded ordnance. We got to know them very well. Two had been engineers in Kabul; another had been an agricultural specialist.

For these particular women, adjusting to life in Pakistan was very difficult. Kabul must have been fairly liberal for an educated woman, but in Pakistan there were much stricter codes – dressing in full-length robes, for example, even in the 50° C heat.

The Afghan people were extremely pleased to have us there. They were honoured that women would actually leave their homes, leave their husbands, and come all this way to help them. The reception wasn't quite so pleasant in the bazaar. The men there were incredibly curious about us. They would follow us, stare at us, sometimes try to bump into us.

Apart from that, there was no real sense of danger. The biggest hazard was the driving. Getting to work was the big event of the day. One morning we came to a bridge that was all backed up. Since we couldn't cross, our driver promptly turned off the road, drove down the bank, across the riverbed – which luckily happened to be dry – and then up the other side.

To them that was an absolutely normal way of driving. We just had our fingers crossed that the car wouldn't hit a huge pothole and break down. We were in uniform and our elbows were showing. That would not have been at all appropriate, having bare arms in public.

The worst part for me was coming back home to Canada – the reverse culture shock. You'd see people worrying about their cars, their televisions, their VCRs, and you'd be thinking: twenty-four hours ago I was in a place where people were worrying about how to feed their children. Here we have so much. It makes some things seem so petty. There they have upwards of thirty languages; here we have trouble with two. It puts your life into perspective when you've been in a situation like that.

Captain Wolfe served in 1990 with the last Canadian team assigned to Operation Salaam, a UN humanitarian assistance program for Afghan refugees.

AFRICA

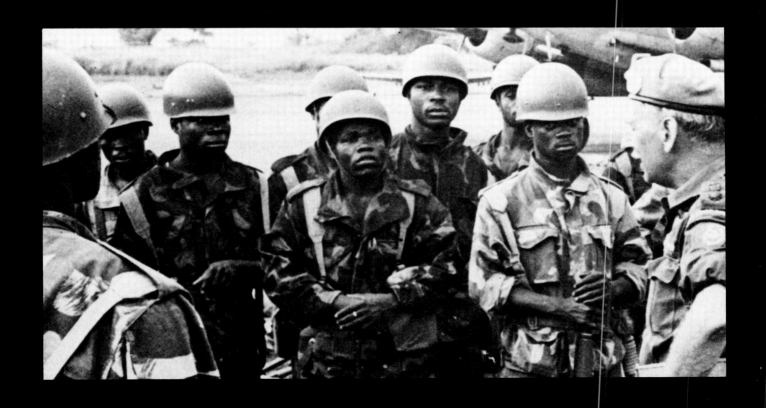

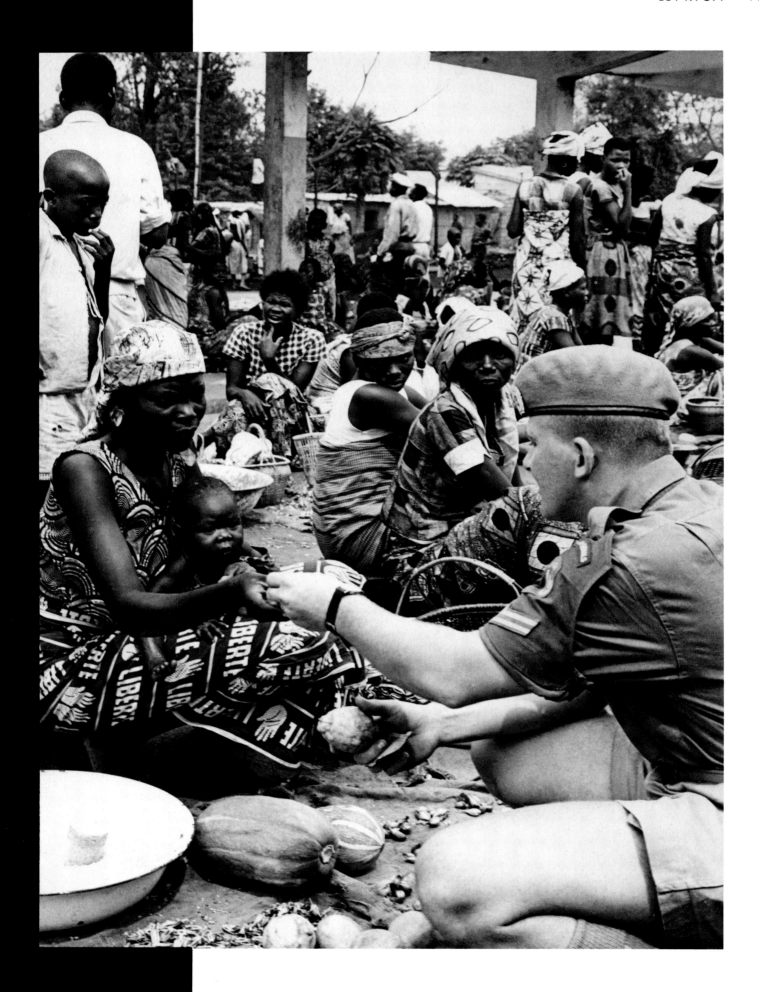

Painstaking last-minute maintenance readies a Canadian Forces Caribou, already painted with the highly visible UN markings, for the long flight from Toronto's Downsview base to the ONUC operation in the troubled Congo.

IF ASIA WAS *TERRA INCOGNITA* for Canadians, so too was Africa. Aside from missionaries and a few colonial-era adventurers, Canadians had paid little attention to events there. The era of decolonization that began early in the 1950s, and accelerated with blinding speed as the 1960s arrived, changed that.

The Belgian Congo (today called Zaïre) was a vast, rich territory that had been a fiefdom of the Belgian monarchy. The heritage was one of cruelty and exploitation, belatedly replaced by paternalism. By the mid-1950s nationalism had begun to develop in the Congo, and riots became more and more frequent. Fearing the costs of a long colonial war that far-sighted politicians in Brussels realized they were bound to lose, Belgium offered independence. Many Belgians agreed to stay on to help administer the country. Elections in May 1960 produced a government headed by Patrice Lumumba that took office on June 30.

But when the black army mutinied against its white officers, the country's inexperienced leaders proved powerless to control the situation, and virtually all the Belgians who had planned to stay fled the country in fear. Brussels sent in tough paratroops to restore order. Within weeks the mineral-rich province of Katanga declared its independence. Lumumba's government, clinging to power desperately, called on the United Nations for help.

The peacekeeping force, called the Opération des Nations Unies au Congo (ONUC), was to help establish order and to ensure the withdrawal of Belgian forces. Initially conceived of as a small advisory body, with its first officers provided from UNTSO in the Middle East, ONUC grew quickly as the magnitude of the problems became obvious. By mid-August there were some 15,000 UN troops there from twenty-four countries; at its peak, ONUC was to number 20,000.

Initially, Canada showed no enthusiasm for participation in ONUC. The government of John Diefenbaker was trying to deal with a difficult domestic economic situation, and the armed forces were short of troops and specialists. But the

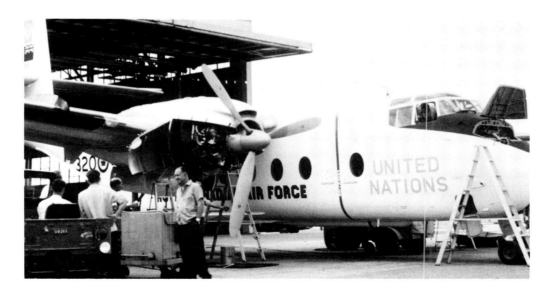

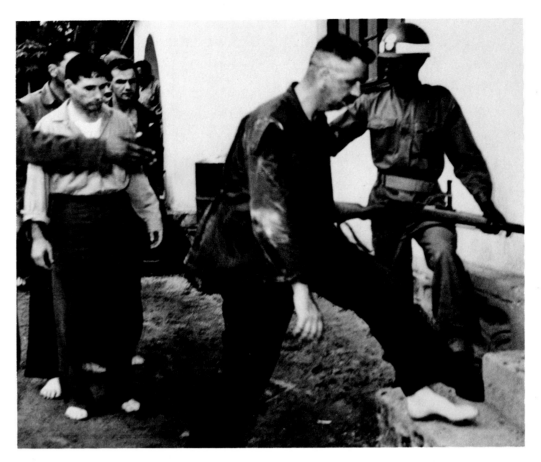

When Canadian peace-keepers arrived in the Congo in August 1960, they were accused of being Belgian by Congolese troops. Some were stripped and beaten; others were jailed. Official apologies followed, but the incidents continued until Canada promised tough retaliation.

requests from New York increased almost daily, and press and public pressure to participate was very strong in Canada. Peacekeeping had become Canadian, and the government could not resist. By late July, Canada had agreed to provide a signals squadron of some 280 officers and men, and these troops, who began to leave for the Congo on August 9, were eventually joined by air units and other technicians and staff officers, to a peak strength of 421.

That this duty was to be no bed of roses became almost instantly clear. Two signals detachments were at Léopoldville's airport on August 18, preparing to fly to their posts, when troops of the Armée Nationale Congolaise (ANC) declared them to be Belgians. At gunpoint, the signallers were stripped and beaten: they were saved from an uncertain fate only by the intervention of Ghanaian ONUC forces who restored order and freed them. Despite stern diplomatic protests from Ottawa to President Lumumba, there would be similar – and worse – incidents in the coming months. In March 1961, after repeated brushes with the ANC, the Canadians finally received orders to shoot to kill if anyone attempted to disarm them.

Fortunately, Canadians were spared the heavy casualties suffered by ONUC infantry, fighting the UN's first peacekeeping war, as they crushed Katangan separatism and fought the mercenary army employed by the breakaway state.

For the Canadians, the task was to provide ONUC's critical communications.

The headquarters for the signal unit was in Léopoldville (now Kinshasa), while detachments, each staffed by an officer and nine men, were scattered throughout the country. Using American radios with a normal range of 400 kilometres, the signallers operated circuits with ranges from 800 to 2,500 kilometres; frequent communications breakdowns were the result. As road and rail communications had collapsed, and as air links were difficult – until Canadian air force officers installed system and regularity into ONUC's air operations – the signallers' role was especially vital. They handled their task superbly.

Individual Canadians demonstrated great bravery. Lieutenant-Colonel Paul Mayer and Sergeant J.A. Lessard won the George Medal for their courageous role in rescuing more than a hundred missionaries from a mob in early 1964. Lieutenant Terry Liston risked his life to rescue a wounded ANC soldier lying in the middle of a minefield, and was made a Member of the Order of the British Empire. But for most Canadians in ONUC the job was prosaic, and the conditions were unpleasant.

By the beginning of 1963, New York had begun planning to wind down ONUC – the expensive nature of the operation was draining the UN's finances. On June 30, 1964, the last 56 Canadians departed for home.

Four years later, Canada had a small role in Nigeria, then fighting a civil war against the secessionist state of Biafra. The war – and the plight of starving Biafrans – attracted huge attention in Canada until Nigeria succeeded in reimposing its authority. But very little of that attention focused on the Observer Team to Nigeria (OTN), dispatched to report on the conduct of Nigerian troops. Two Canadian officers served in Nigeria as part of this twelve-man team.

Two decades later, Canada agreed to contribute observers to UNAVEM, the Portuguese acronym for the UN Angola Verification Mission – a force set up in 1988 to preside over the end of a long civil war in the former Portuguese colony in south-west Africa. Cuban troops, acting as Soviet surrogates, fought against South African units, while two indigenous political movements and their armies clashed. The end of the Cold War, the withdrawal of the foreign contingents, and weariness with the war led to a settlement, but UNAVEM remains in place.

Canada's next major contribution to peacekeeping in Africa took place in Namibia, the former South West Africa. Controlled by the Republic of South Africa, which had inherited the German mandate over the territory after the First World War, South West Africa had been ruled from Pretoria. Repeated UN efforts to force the South Africans to give up the colony were rebuffed, and inevitably guerrillas – the South West Africa People's Organization, or SWAPO – took the field. After a long struggle and difficult negotiations in which Canada played a major part, the South Africans gave ground, and the UN established the United Nations Transition Assistance Group (UNTAG) at the beginning of 1989 to

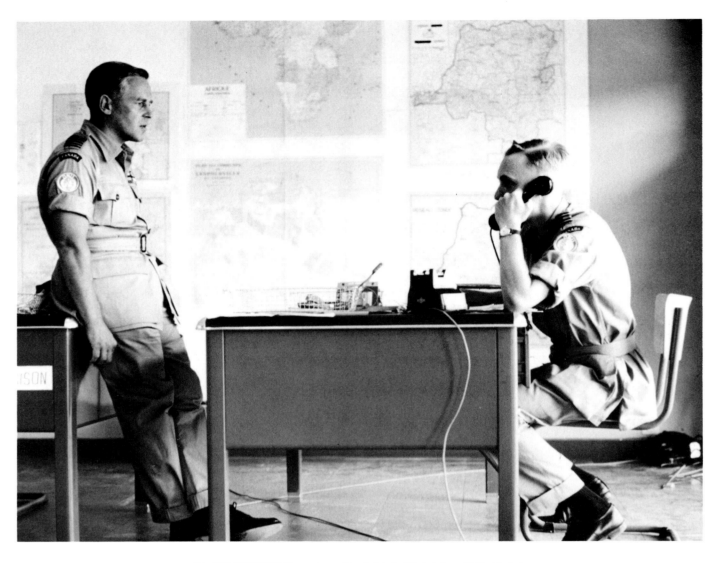

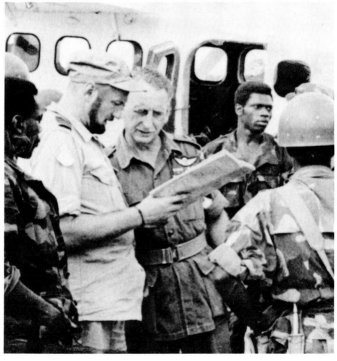

ABOVE:

The barebones operational room of ONUC at Leopoldville, in 1960. Journalist Peter Worthington described the Canadians as friendly and capable but distinctly scruffy: "the only creases the trousers hold in the steambath climate are wrinkles."

Lt.-Col. Mayer, a Swedish pilot, and Congolese paratroopers prepare to leave on a mercy mission to evacuate over 100 missionaries being threatened by a violent mob in Kisandji. Mayer received the George Medal for his part in the rescue.

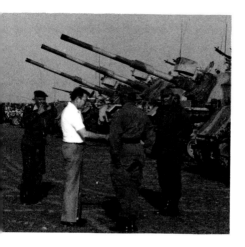

In 1988, Maj.-Gen. Terence Liston led a UN technical survey to the Western Sahara, seeking a ceasefire and referendum between Morocco and the Polisario guerrillas. Three years later the UN authorized intervention by a new operation, MINURSO.

supervise free elections.

Although military personnel took part, Canada's major contribution to UNTAG was a hundred volunteers from the Royal Canadian Mounted Police. Sent over in October 1989 and wearing tropical khaki instead of their usual woollen uniforms, the Mounties worked with the local police, gradually building relationships of trust. Their task was to ensure that the elections and the policing of them were fair, and to do so they manned polling stations, guarded ballot boxes, and went on patrol with the local force. The elections were duly certified as free and fair, with SWAPO emerging as a clear winner. UNTAG had done its task well; so had the Mounties.

Next came MINURSO, the UN Mission for the Referendum in Western Sahara. Authorized by the UN in the spring of 1991, this peacekeeping force – to which Canada had promised the force commander and a battalion of infantry – has been desperately slow to get into operation. Local hostility, climate, poor sanitation – a host of difficulties have prevented MINURSO from supervising the referendum intended to end the war between the Polisario guerrillas and Morocco. At this writing, just over 300 UN blue berets, including 34 Canadian officers and other ranks, are on site. The promised infantry battalion, Canada's main contribution, has been ready and waiting to go since the late summer of 1991, but continues to stew at home while the UN tries to build a few bridges between the antagonists. Until that can be done, peacekeeping efforts are not only futile but dangerous.

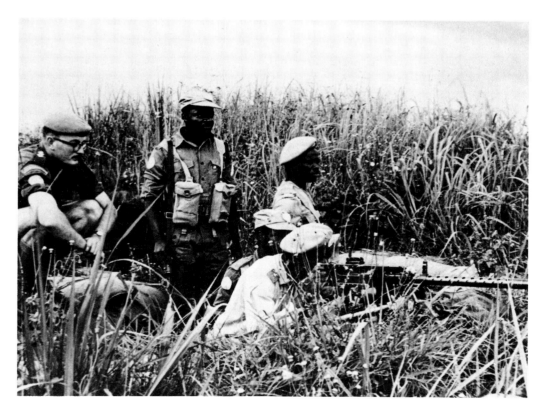

"Military people have a lot in common, even when they come from different ends of the world," says Maj.-Gen. Terence Liston (*far left*), here examining a Congolese machine gun position in 1962. "You develop an empathy for the other guy very, very quickly."

CHAOS IN KABONGO

MAJOR-GENERAL TERENCE LISTON

Congo

The Congo was my first peacekeeping experience, my first time out of the country. It was the end of 1962 and I was a young lieutenant.

Getting to Léopoldville, the capital, took a couple of days back then. We flew over the Alps in an unpressurized North Star, with what looked like giant condoms over our faces for oxygen, covered in grey blankets, with newspapers on the floor to keep our feet from freezing.

Coming from a French-speaking regiment, I was able to use what was then the lingua franca in many parts of the country. Before long I was sent to join a Congolese battalion, the one that had sparked the rebellion against the Belgians. I was their liaison with the UN. I lived with them, moved with them in the bush.

At first these people seemed very, very different . . . the tribal scars, the tattoos, the curious things some of them had done with their teeth. But after the initial shock wore off, I found they were just guys like I had known back home. It sounds corny, but I developed a tremendous feeling of brotherhood living out there with them.

After several months we found ourselves in a little place called Kabongo. The village was completely empty. What we didn't know was that Kabongo's waterhole had been completely surrounded with mines. That's what was keeping the inhabitants from returning.

As our soldiers got to the edge of the waterhole there was an explosion. Other Congolese hurried back to get me. They told me about the minefield. They had no idea what to do. I went down and saw what had happened.

As a young officer cadet at Borden, I'd gone through this very drill – how to get yourself through a minefield. I got down on my hands and knees and started looking, probing with a bayonet. I didn't have to think. I knew exactly what to do, just as I'd been trained.

The men weren't a great distance, maybe ten metres

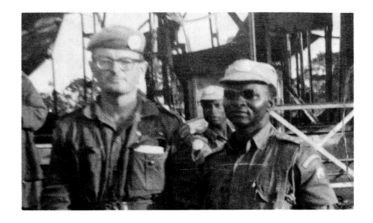

Congolese troops couldn't understand why the village at Kabongo had been deserted by its civilian population. The reason: rebels had mined the waterhole. When two Congolese soldiers became trapped in the minefield, Lieutenant Liston crawled forward and pulled them out.

into the minefield. When I got to them, one of the soldiers was already dead. The other guy was still alive and I pulled him out, but he was in pretty rough shape. We had no doctor, and in a couple of hours he died as well.

It wasn't a very dramatic event, except for me personally and for the guys involved. It just came to me and I had to do it. I'd never have been able to go home and face my regiment if I had not performed well when faced with a crisis. But in terms of the demands made on people in times of war, it was nothing more than a passing incident.

I learned something very important in the Congo. I saw good food, sent by aid organizations, rotting on the docks. I saw fields with wonderfully fertile soil, unplanted. The problem in the Congo was not the lack of potential for feeding people. It was the chaos caused by fighting. This is the great satisfaction for the UN peacekeeper – knowing that by bringing about stability, you also help bring about self-sufficiency.

In recognition of his actions, Major-General Liston was named a Member of the Order of the British Empire.

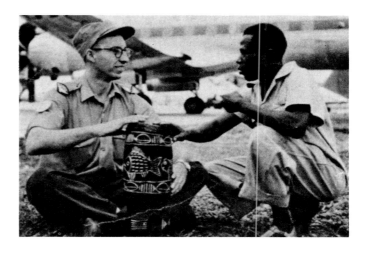

TARZAN ENGLISH

CORPORAL ROGER CYR

Congo

It was July 11, 1960. I'd just walked into my flight sergeant's office. "Go home and get your things together," he told me. "You're leaving for the Congo." The Congo, I thought, now where in hell is that? Five days later, I was on the job in Léopoldville.

I was a safety systems non-commissioned officer in the Royal Canadian Air Force. One of my jobs was replenishing the oxygen system before aircraft returned to Canada for more UN troops and equipment. The first day there, someone told me I could find a supply of oxygen at a hangar a short distance from ours.

Walking into the building, I came on a large black man. I knew this was to be expected. After all, we were in Africa, right? My only problem was how to make this fellow understand what I wanted.

I didn't know much about that part of the world. A few Tarzan movies was about my limit. I walked up to this fellow, holding my right hand up Indian-style, and said something like: "Bwana. Me Canada. Need oxygen. You have?"

He glanced up from his work with a curious look but didn't speak. Realizing he couldn't understand, I held both arms out like wings and circled the office, making the noise of an aircraft engine. "Need oxygen," I kept

"The Congo. Now where the hell is that?" Despite a shaky start, the beat of a foreign culture captivated Cpl. Roger Cyr, a safety systems expert stationed in Léopoldville with ONUC.

repeating. "For big silver bird."

He tolerated a few more minutes of this, then leaned back in his chair. "Just what is it you want, sir?" he asked. "And what language do you speak?"

"Oh, English," I stammered. "And a little French."

"Well," he replied, "I speak seven languages myself. So pick either of the two that you know, and maybe we can talk."

We agreed on English. "I'll have one of my men meet your aircraft every day to look after your needs," he promised as I left the hangar. "Oh, and son – you've seen one Tarzan movie too many."

Corporal Cyr returned home in September of 1960, once the airlift of UN troops from Canada to the Congo was completed.

FIRST OF JULY

MAJOR SHELAGH STEVENS

Namibia

It was a standard UN operation, as much as you can call any UN operation standard. Namibia is the size of a large Canadian province, quite an area when you have troops spread throughout. The mission carried flags of five colours, representing the five different continents

involved. It was truly an international peacekeeping operation. There were press people from everywhere, covering the elections.

We went in prepared for the worst. We'd had shots for every possible illness. On top of that, we'd been warned about the poisonous snakes, and issued snakebite kits. So the moment we stepped off the plane we were on our guard.

Problem was, it had been quite a long flight. We

were exhausted. Our transportation wasn't there, so we had a couple of hours to kill. In the airport washroom the first thing we noticed was the beetles. They were the size of your fist! If those were the beetles, we were in no hurry to see the snakes.

There we sat, in the heat, surrounded by journalists, on constant watch for those terrible snakes. Naturally they never gave us any problems. As time went by we forgot all about them.

It was fascinating country. I ate crocodile, springbok, and ostrich. I was able to see some spectacular wildlife in my spare time. But you really looked forward to those letters from home. In a situation like that, mail is incredibly important. My mother was so supportive. She'd send care packages, and they'd be devoured before I even left the mess.

One perhaps unusual thing about Namibia was that all who served there seemed quite pleased, not to say surprised, that it went so well. The UN was there to supervise the elections, assist in the transition of power, and then leave. And it actually worked out that way. It was a nice feather in the cap for the peacekeepers.

I think most Canadians are quietly nationalistic. But when you are in a situation like that, you realize how exceptionally lucky you are. I never celebrated Canada Day at home with the same spirit I did when I was away. On the first of July, or whenever you saw our flag waving over an embassy, you couldn't help feeling really proud to be a Canadian.

Finance officer for the Canadian contingent of the UN Transition Assistance Group, Major Stevens was headquartered in Windhoek, Namibia's capital, from 1989 to 1990.

TOTALLY AWED

BOMBARDIER BERNARD ATKINSON
Namibia

I spent a month in northern Namibia, up along the Angolan border. Pretty rugged terrain. Drove over 1,600 kilometres and went through twenty-seven tires in thirty days.

Part of my job was taking care of two UN representatives there to monitor the elections. One was from Hungary, the other from Russia. The Hungarian was a policeman. He came in full uniform, a heavy cotton camouflage, very hot for that weather. The other fellow, the Russian, dressed in a suit and tie.

They had never camped out before. The first time we stopped, I had to show them how to erect their tent, how to set up the cots, basically teach them how to live out in the woods. At night I would collect the wood, get a fire going, start the Coleman stove, get the food on.

The important thing was choosing the right spot to pitch camp. Clearings were best. You wouldn't want to sleep under a tree, not with some of the snakes they have there. And you'd keep away from the rocky areas, because that's where the scorpions were worst. But as long as you stayed fairly close together and kept the fire going, you'd be fine.

We saw lots of wildlife. There were elephants, crocodiles, grasshoppers three times the size we see in Canada. The UN guys were totally awed by it. As was I.

It was a real adventure. Plus, you felt like you were doing something good. The people there were finally getting some say in their own government.

Bombardier Atkinson was posted to Opuwo, Namibia, with the UN Transition Assistance Group. He provided transportation services throughout the Kaoko Veld.

CYPRUS

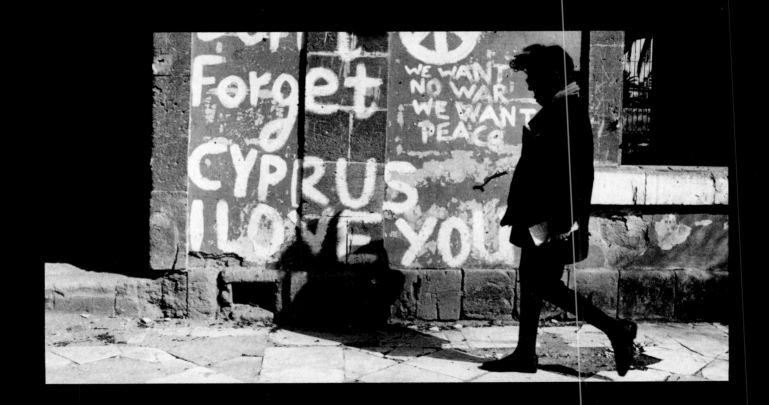

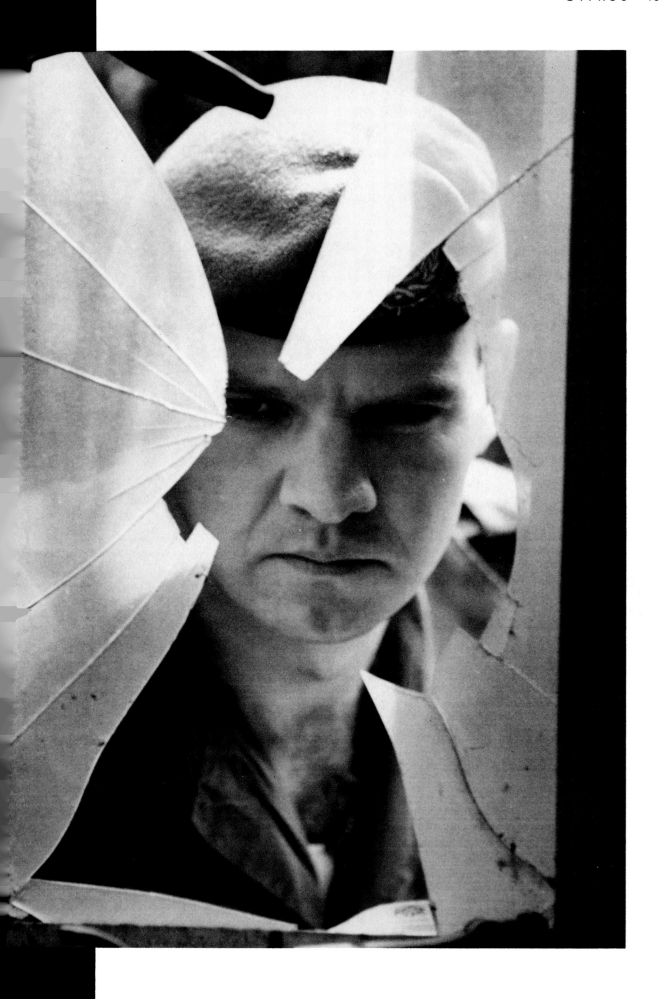

SOME UNITED NATIONS PEACEKEEPING operations begin in hope, continue in frustration, and seem they will never end. One of them is UNFICYP, the United Nations Force in Cyprus. There are lesser operations that have had longer lives, but UNFICYP is the only large force to have remained in place for close to thirty years.

A small island in the eastern Mediterranean, Cyprus has a population of just under three-quarters of a million; 80 percent are of Greek origin and the remainder are of Turkish descent. The island was a British colony until 1959, when it won its independence after a long political and guerrilla struggle. The Treaty of Guarantee that sanctioned the new republic's independence obliged Britain, Greece, and Turkey to uphold the country's security, but gave each the right of unilateral action to restore the conditions to those in existence in 1959. Each power had the right to station troops on the island, as well.

By 1963, this unwieldy structure was on the verge of toppling. The Cypriot president, Archbishop Makarios, seemed prepared to change the constitution in ways that would enhance the power of the Greek Cypriots and menace the Turkish minority. That led to riots that threatened to escalate and to military moves in Turkey. It did not take long for Britain to suggest that a peacekeeping force from NATO, to which both Greece and Turkey belonged, might be the answer. Makarios's response was a cool one, and the British then suggested a Commonwealth peacekeeping operation instead. Makarios insisted that only a UN force would be acceptable, and in March 1964 the Security Council duly authorized UNFICYP's establishment.

Canada had been suggested for membership in both the NATO and Commonwealth forces, and its presence was similarly considered essential in the UN force. Indeed, Prime Minister Lester Pearson and his Secretary of State for External Affairs, Paul Martin, played critical roles in setting up UNFICYP and securing commitments from other contributors in a hectic few days of telephone calls and arm-twisting. This effort was not universally hailed in Canada; some Quebec newspapers harked back to the South African War of 1899 and suggested that Canada was being asked yet again to pull Britain's chestnuts from the fire. The English-language press was scarcely more enthusiastic.

But Ottawa persisted. Fearing that a Turkish invasion of Cyprus might lead to a Greco-Turkish war and the splintering of NATO's southern front, Canada put a battalion of the Royal 22e Régiment (the "Van Doos", the designated stand-by battalion for UN service at the time), and a squadron of armoured cars of the Royal Canadian Dragoons aboard Royal Canadian Air Force transports and HMCS *Bonaventure*, the navy's sole aircraft carrier. They were sped to Cyprus, where they were the first and, for some time, the only UN forces. The invasion

PAGE 108:

The stalemate in Cyprus has gone on for almost 40 years.

PREVIOUS PAGE:

Maj. Yvan Bouchard of Anse St. Jean, Saguenay Lac-St. Jean, looks through a broken window in the deserted French embassy on the "green line" in Nicosia.

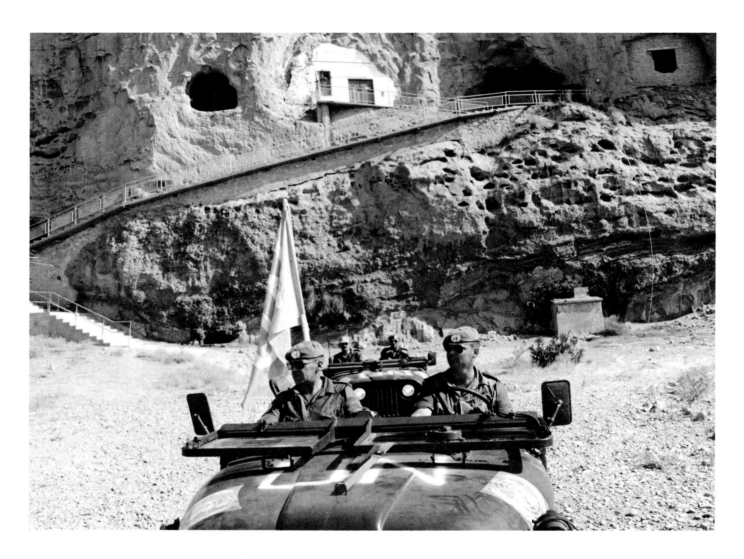

threat dissipated, and the Canadian peacekeepers – soon joined by Sweden, Finland, Denmark, Ireland, and other contributors, to a total strength of 6,500 – began patrolling the tense communal boundaries.

Canada's 1,150 soldiers initially had the most difficult task – guarding the "Green Line" that divided the Greek and Turkish districts of the capital, Nicosia. Section and platoon patrols proved insufficient to deter full-scale attacks by the Greek Cypriots and retaliatory air strikes by the Turkish air force. After the Van Doos took fire from both sides of the line, the Canadians, following a new policy of "diplomatic toughness", won permission to create a physical neutral zone by clearing houses and shops on both sides and interposing their companies between the fractious Cypriots. In December 1964, other UNFICYP units took over the Nicosia duty, and the Canadians shifted their operations to the road between Nicosia and the port of Kyrenia. For a time, at least, they were successful in winning friends – a poll of Greek Cypriot schoolchildren showed that the Canadians were just behind the Irish and tied with the Finns as the most popular UNFICYP contingent!

Bleached by centuries of Cyprian sun, a cliffside monastery looks over the latest visitors in the island's long and often volatile history. Watching, reporting, and mediating, Canadians have helped keep the peace on Cyprus since 1964.

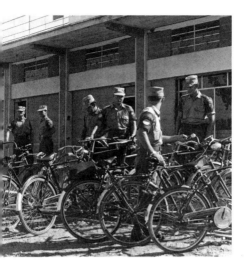

Mobile patrol in the sensitive Nicosia area calls for equal measures of diplomacy and stamina. These bicycles parked in front of a mess hall in the suburbs in 1971 provided quiet, surprisingly flexible transportation through the city's narrow streets.

By the end of 1964, while a settlement was as much a dream as ever, tension had lessened, and Canada began to rotate its units regularly, adopting a six-month tour of duty as the norm. But UNFICYP continued to be essential to both sides, and although the Canadian contingent was cut in half in 1969, no progress towards settlement had been made. In 1974, a military junta, pledged to bring about a union of Cyprus and Greece, seized power in Athens, and toppled the Makarios government. The Turks responded by invading the island, sending 40,000 tough soldiers ashore and causing a massive movement of refugees. Cyprus was now effectively divided into separate Greek and Turkish enclaves.

For UNFICYP the Turkish invasion proved to be the worst of times. The UN in New York had few suggestions for the peacekeeping force, merely telling UNFICYP to do its best. The Canadians and their colleagues did that, determining to minimize casualties to themselves and to fulfil such humanitarian tasks as they could. This was no easy chore. The Airborne Regiment, Canada's contingent in 1974, dug in, suffered some casualties, and tried to preserve what it could. Canadians distinguished themselves by rescuing women and children hostages and by keeping the Nicosia airport and other sites as neutral zones. One officer, Captain Alain Forand, won Canada's Star of Courage for rescuing under fire two Canadians wounded by Greek Cypriots. His comrades knocked out the machine-gun post that had done the damage and provided covering fire for Forand's mercy mission. The Canadian army's patience, in other words, was not unlimited.

The 1974 crisis led Canada to double its contingent. This time, heavier weapons came along to help UNFICYP create and preserve a buffer zone running the entire length of the island. Even today, neither side accepts this buffer easily; the Turkish Cypriots see it as a dead zone open only to UNFICYP, while the Greek Cypriots persist in the position that it is their territory, temporarily administered by UNFICYP. The result is persistent tension, frequent outbursts of gunfire, and enormous stress for the blue-helmeted peacekeepers.

A Canadian-manned observation post is threatened by Turks, who have planted their flag alongside it.

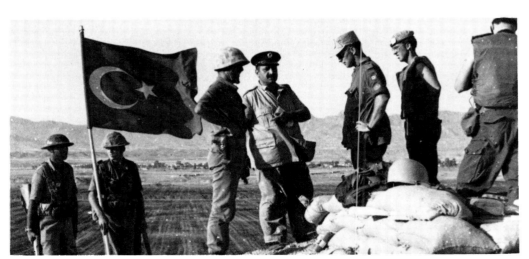

Walking a careful line, Canadians in Cyprus patrol the country's most contentious area – the buffer zone dissecting the capital city, Nicosia. The "green line", an arbitrary border between Greek and Turkish Cypriots sometimes only metres apart, gives UN peace-keepers little breathing-space in which to operate.

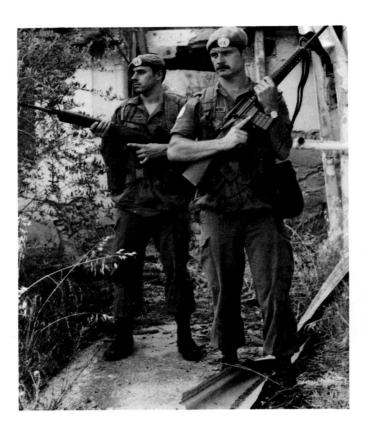

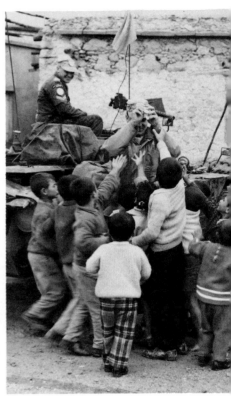

After almost thirty years of UN efforts, the situation continues in frozen hostility. Both sides arm themselves to the teeth, purchasing ever-heavier weaponry and training National Guards that become more professional every day. Meanwhile, the human and fiscal costs of UNFICYP continue to climb. Twenty-seven Canadians have died on UNFICYP duty, most, but not all, in accidents. The total cost of UNFICYP to date is more than $2 billion and the annual budget is more than $100 million. Given the UN's financial difficulties and the reluctance of many members to pay their share of the costs, the burden of supporting UNFICYP inevitably falls on the countries contributing troops.

Is it worth it? As time passes it becomes harder to give an unequivocal affirmative response. The peace has been kept, after a fashion, but there has been no progress whatsoever towards a permanent settlement. Still, there has been no all-out war between Greece and Turkey, and that is a blessing. Cyprus has provided a good training ground for Canadian soldiers, who have learned small-unit tactics in a working laboratory. On the other hand, our limited infantry forces are stretched very thin, and some Canadians have served six, seven, or eight six-month tours in Cyprus. Repeated separations from family and friends are hard to take.

In 1992 Canada and the other UNFICYP members began to insist that the Cypriots and their backers settle the issue, and in May of that year Canada warned that it was contemplating a phased withdrawal unless progress was made. What the outcome will be remains unclear.

An appreciative crowd in Aya Irini, a small village on the north-west coast of Cyprus, surrounds a Canadian. This is an experience familiar to peacekeepers around the world. In fact, many have learned to restrict handouts to small souvenirs and food. Gifts of money are often channelled through Forces-organized community projects.

THE TOLL OF ANGER

MAJOR ALLAN ALEXANDER

Cyprus

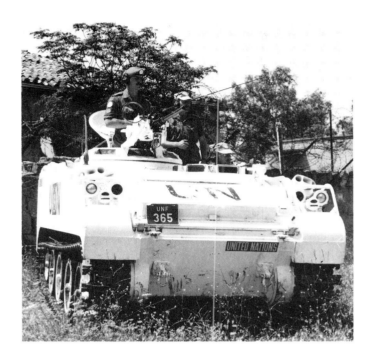

In the early days of the Cyprus conflict, we patrolled the Kyrenian Mountains. There is a castle there, one of the castles Walt Disney used in some of his films, and it overlooks and controls both sides of the mountain. The Greek Cypriots had held it for some time, but then Turkish Cypriots climbed up commando-fashion and took it over.

One day as my patrol was passing, the Greek Cypriots mounted an attack to take the castle back. We were caught in the middle. Both sides were shooting at each other, dropping mortars. And there we were, in no man's land, trying to negotiate a peaceful end to the problem.

That's peacekeeping. Often you just find yourself in the middle. Your mandate is to help prevent more fighting. That doesn't mean you stand up and wave a blue flag and yell, "Stop." That can be dangerous to your continued health. In fact, your first reaction is to get the hell out of there.

But hopefully, the people you are mediating with see you as an honest broker. They know you are trying to enforce agreements their leaders have agreed on. Of course, there always is the danger they will ignore your good intentions. In that case, you have to be prepared to back up your words.

Despite all the shooting, we never had anyone hurt by weapons fire. Our casualties were all from accidents. We lost one trooper when his armoured scout car tried to avoid hitting a lady and a donkey on a mountain pass. He took the wrong side of the road, the car flipped over the side of the mountain, and he was killed.

Peacekeeping jobs are always hardest on the families, the ones left behind. My wife knows it's something I have to do. I don't say she looks forward to it, but it's part of the

"You never wanted to use your weapons," says Maj. Alexander, who served in Cyprus in 1964, "but when you need firepower to prevent further violence, you've got to have sufficient force. And both sides have to know it." Today that situation has changed little – especially on the "green line", where this Lynx is used as a mobile observation post.

military career. When you do come back, picking up the pieces is hard, too. You have to recognize you are no longer the head of the household. I don't think you ever regain that spot. Once your spouse has survived without you for six months or a year, your marriage changes. You both become more mature, more capable.

The futility of the destruction and the killing you witness as a peacekeeper is frustrating. And no, we haven't stopped it. But we've done what we were sent to do. We've minimized a lot of hardship, a lot of death. Reduced the toll of anger.

It's always nice to come back to Canada. But peacekeeping somehow just gets into your blood.

Major Alexander served with the first Canadian contingent to Cyprus in 1964.

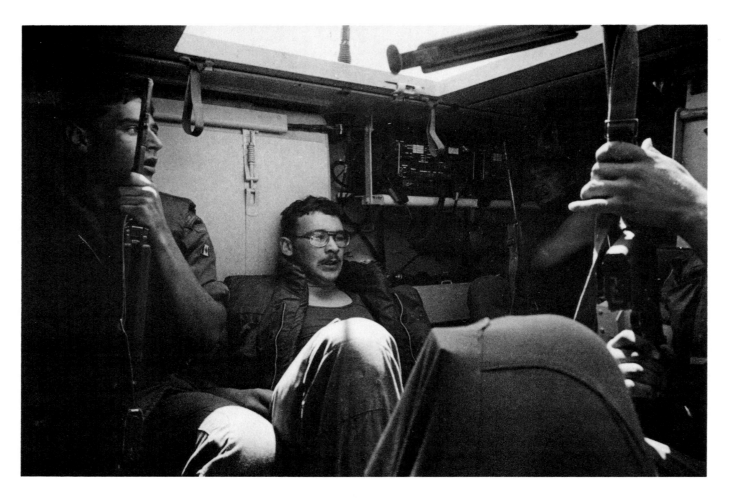

COURAGE UNDER FIRE

Colonel Alain Forand
Major Normand Blaquière
Corporal Michael Plouffe
Cyprus

FORAND:

When I served in Cyprus in 1969, we were a very young organization. I had men in my platoon who were eighteen and nineteen. One of my biggest fears was that I would have trouble controlling their enthusiasm. But I found that when a problem arose those guys were like veterans, just like their ancestors in the first and second world wars. It was fantastic the way they turned into professionals, adapting to circumstances.

By my second tour, in 1974, the situation in Cyprus had grown more tense. There were conflicts between the Greek and the Turkish Cypriots every day, fighting right

The strain of renewed violence shows in the faces of Canadians taking temporary shelter in an armoured car during the 1974 Turkish invasion of Cyprus. Though the peacekeepers undoubtedly saved many lives, both warring sides would fight around, over, and through UN positions.

in the heart of Nicosia. At some locations the combatants were no more than a hundred metres apart.

On July 23 I received a report of shelling in the north-west part of town. A Canadian post was situated there, along with a medical station. Apparently they had come under mortar fire from Turkish Cypriots who were trying to reach a nearby Greek Cypriot position.

BLAQUIÈRE:

It was a sunny afternoon when the Turkish Cypriots attacked the Greek Cypriot–held prison near our base.

From the prison there was a good vantage overlooking the surrounding countryside.

The Turkish Cypriot ammunition was small calibre, and their equipment was outdated. As a result, many of the shells supposed to hit the prison fell short and landed on our barracks.

As soon as the Turkish Cypriots began attacking the prison on foot, the Greek Cypriots opened up with machine-gun fire. They quickly killed many of the attackers. Meanwhile, a mortar shell had started a fire at our base and we scrambled to fight it.

Hidden by the smoke, fifteen or eighteen Turkish Cypriot soldiers escaped the battle and backed off into our camp. They were young and very frightened. The Greek Cypriots saw them retreating into our post, and by megaphone ordered us to eject them or face retaliation.

I managed to convince the Turkish Cypriot sergeant that to remain neutral we had to escort them outside our perimeter. We decided to exit by the rear and cross the Pedieas River to reach Turkish Cypriot territory.

We opened a gate in the fence that surrounded our compound and left with the Turks. On my command everyone was to proceed forward across the river.

PLOUFFE:

I was Captain Blaquière's driver. After the Turks entered our camp he asked me to help escort them out. When we got to the river Captain Blaquière gave the signal and the first group of Turkish Cypriots started across. Captain Blaquière was in the middle; I was off to one side. A few seconds later the Greek Cypriots started firing.

BLAQUIÈRE:

I crossed the river – more of a creek, really – with the first group. But the rest took longer to catch up and they were caught in the Greek Cypriot fire.

Using a megaphone, I tried to find out what had happened to Private Plouffe and the others. I couldn't hear what they were saying. Thinking they were injured,

I turned back to help. It was at that point I felt myself hit in both legs. I lost all feeling in my legs but managed to roll down into the river, out of direct fire.

PLOUFFE:

When we heard the machine-gun and assault rifles start firing, we all hit the ground. I took cover behind a Turkish Cypriot who appeared to be dead. Then I heard Captain Blaquière shout, "My leg is broken. I can't feel it."

I crawled over to him and cut his trouser leg with my knife. I could see that the bullet had gone clean through. I used my shell dressing to apply direct pressure. The Greek Cypriots were still shooting.

FORAND:

I arrived at the post driving a Ferret, an armoured vehicle. By that point the medical clinic had burned to the ground. A couple of guys ran up. They told me that at the end of our facility, in the Pedieas River, two of our men were pinned down by a Greek Cypriot machine-gunner.

I learned that our men in the creek bed were Captain Blaquière and Private Plouffe. Blaquière, a good friend of mine, had been hit in the legs. I got there to find Plouffe covering Blaquière with his body.

PLOUFFE:

When Captain Forand arrived, he yelled, "Plouffe, is everything all right?" I lifted my head to reply, and a bullet hit me in the helmet and deflected into my jaw. The force rolled me over onto my back. It gave me a start. I rolled back onto my stomach and heard a rattling noise in my mouth. I spat into my hand and saw a bullet and several bloody teeth. "They should have hit the other side," I told Captain Blaquière, "where I've got a cavity."

BLAQUIÈRE:

Plouffe put the bullet into his pocket. He said, "This will

be a good souvenir," and continued giving me first aid.

FORAND:

In a situation like that you only think about what might happen to the other guys, not to you. These were men from my own unit. I had been together with Blaquière almost since I joined the army. All I knew was that they were in trouble. They had to be extracted as quickly as possible.

I saw the only way I could possibly get into the creek with any chance of coming back was to have some kind of covering firepower. I sent the armoured car over to a position across the creek and had a .50-calibre set up. When they were in place I told the group, "I'm going in. If they start shooting, I want you to answer back."

The Greek Cypriots opened fire as soon as I started down into the creek bed. I crawled forward and helped Captain Blaquière up the bank. Then we got the others.

BLAQUIÈRE:

After I was evacuated I awoke to find myself in a hospital room. There was a Greek Cypriot in the bed on one side, and a Turkish Cypriot on my other side. Plouffe had done such a good job bandaging my leg, the doctor said he couldn't have done better himself.

Thinking about it later, I realized I was the only one in that group crossing the river wearing a blue beret. From their angle the Greek Cypriots could probably only see a bunch of Turkish Cypriots running towards the river. I was in the right place at the wrong time.

FORAND:

That's all there was to it. It had to be done, so we got on with it. We had that reputation. As Canadians we were known for getting the job done, as people willing to help anywhere it was needed.

The biggest hurdle in a mission like Cyprus is staying flexible, adapting. As a peacekeeper you have to remind yourself to look at things with the eyes of the people living there. You are not there to change them, just to help.

That's the thing I hang my hat on: if not for us, the killing would certainly resume. That gives me quite a bit of satisfaction, knowing we've done what we could. After all, what is more important than preventing the loss of even one life?

For their actions in Cyprus on July 23, 1974, Captain Forand and Private Plouffe were awarded the Star of Courage; Captain Blaquière received the Medal of Bravery.

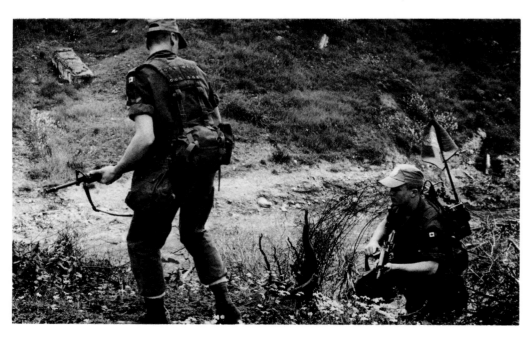

A river with a bloody past, the Pedieas – patrolled by Cpl. Benoit Champagne and Pte. Joel Langlois – was the site of the 1974 incident in which Maj. Normand Blaquière was wounded. "I lost all feeling in my legs," he recalls, "but managed to roll down into the river, out of direct fire."

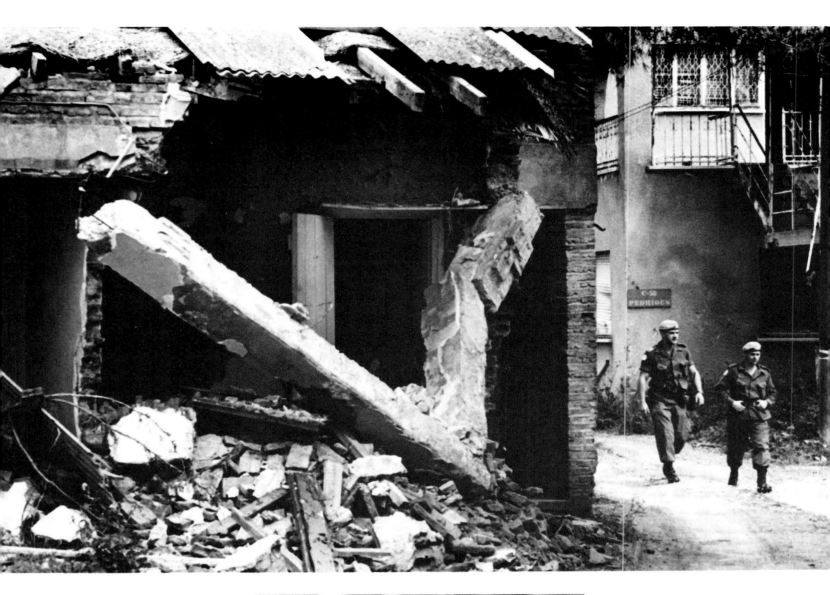

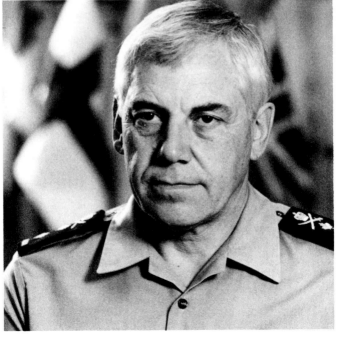

"We are preserving a calm that would not exist without our presence," says Maj.-Gen. Clive Milner, first Canadian to command a UN force in 30 years. "To be in charge of that process is very rewarding."

OPPOSITE AND RIGHT:
Canadian soldiers in
Nicosia: Canada's long-
standing commitment to
the conflict means that
virtually all regular-force
soldiers from the infantry,
artillery, and armoured
corps serve here at some
point in their career.

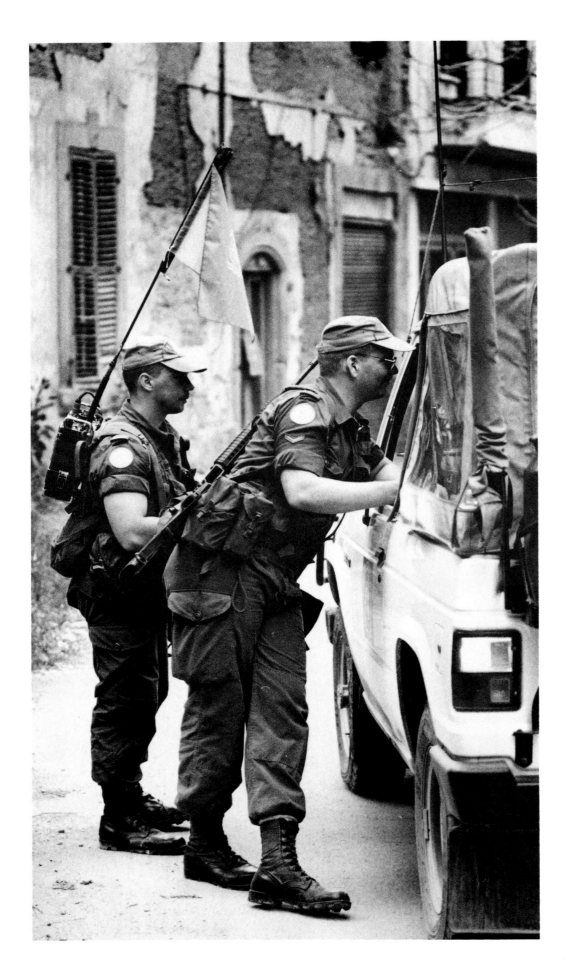

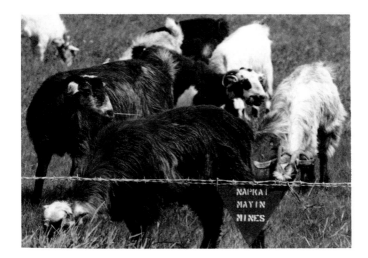

Active minefields in the buffer zone are easy to spot: land with an untended look – tall grass, untilled soil – almost certainly signals uncleared ordnance. But it's tough to convince farmers that land that once was theirs is no longer safe. "I know of one farmer who lowered his tractor into the buffer zone to till the soil," says Capt. Brian Brulotte. "It struck a mine and he was killed."

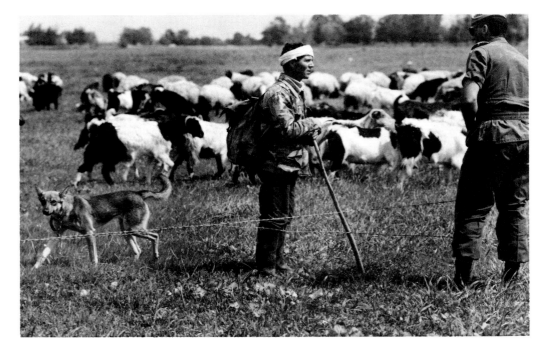

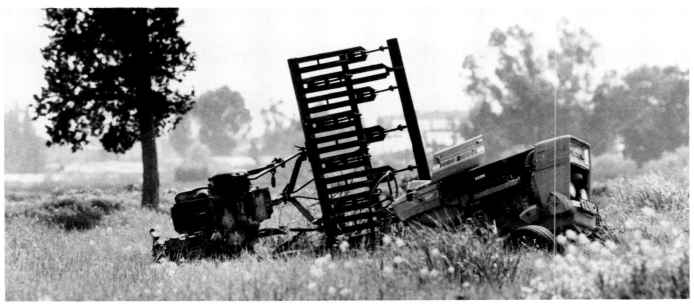

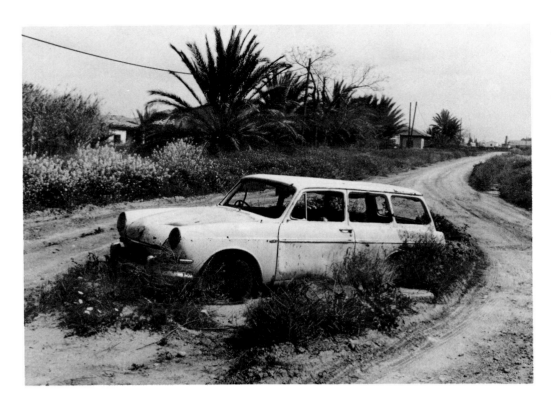

A grim monument to a vividly remembered war, a car in which two Turkish journalists were killed by anti-tank rocket fire in 1974 stands where it was hit. Canadian peacekeepers tried to have it moved off the roadway at the time, but Turkish Cypriots insisted that it remain as a reminder of the incident.

The buffer zone stretches 217 km across the island's middle, a crude slash open only to UN-cleared traffic. It not only displaces residents and homes but also cuts off access to badly needed arable land.

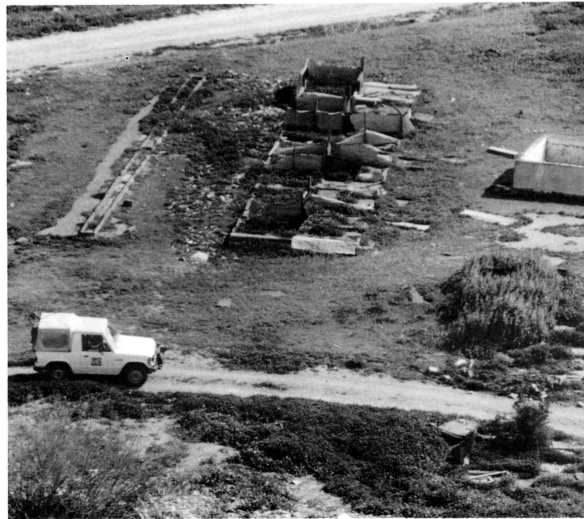

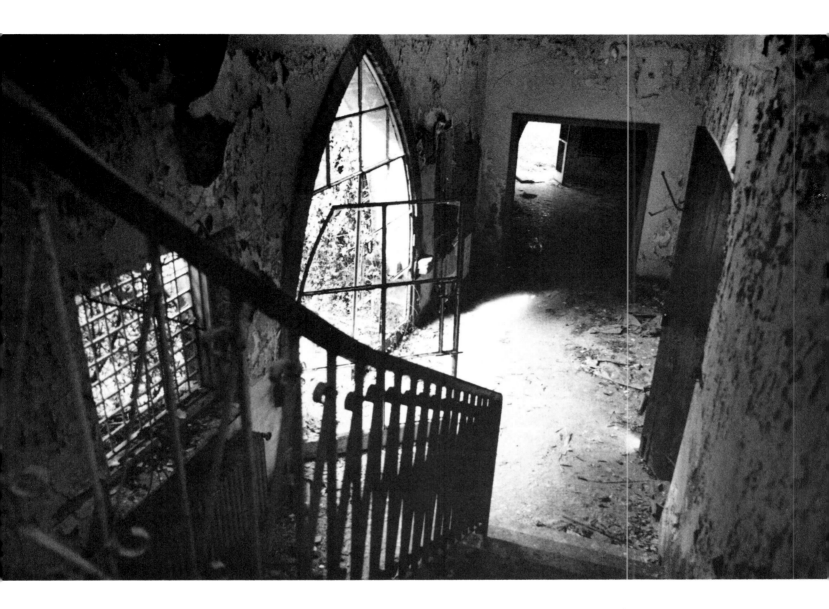

Nicosia's once-gracious French embassy today hosts only UN patrols and the rodents that scuttle through its rooms. Shattered by the fierce battles of 1974, it straddles the no-man's land between Turkish and Greek Cypriot territories.

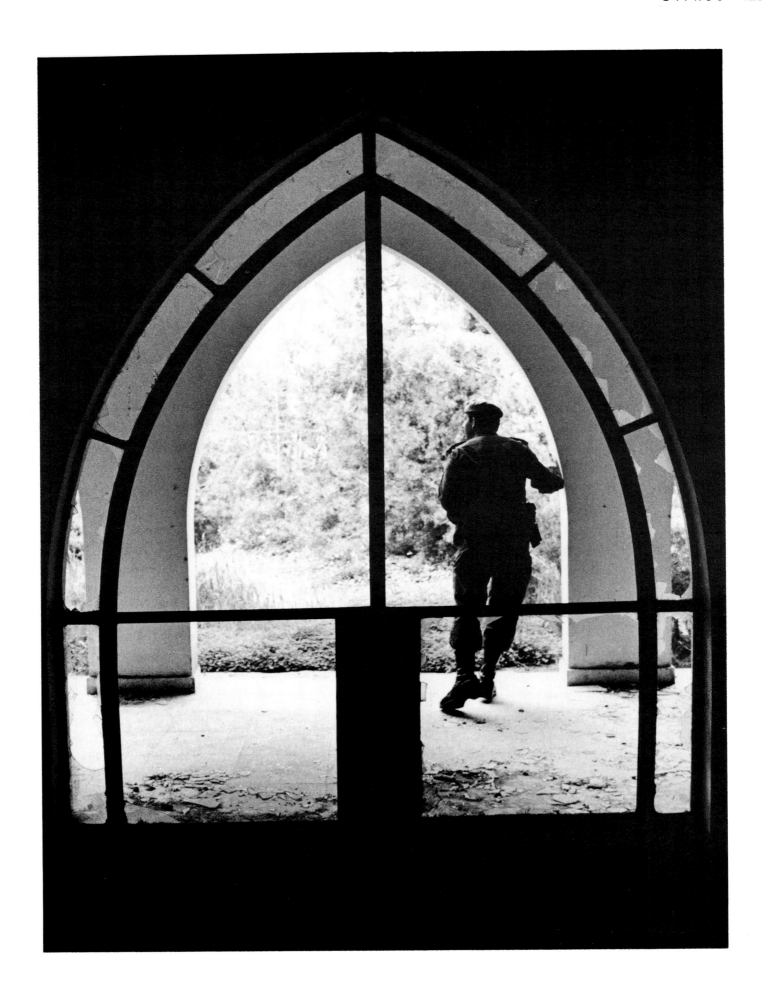

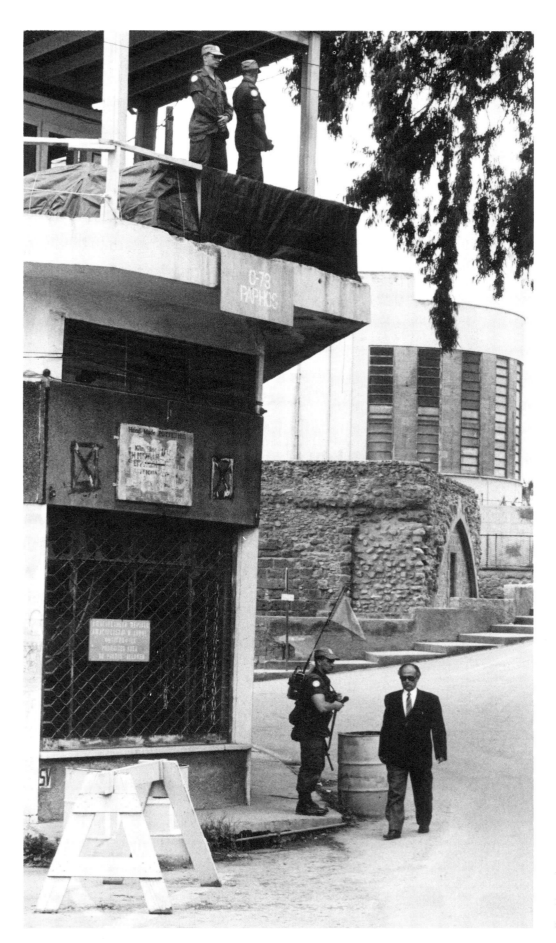

LEFT AND OPPOSITE:
The buffer zone began as
a line drawn on a map in
green pencil; the term
"green line" has now
become a general name
for disputed borders being
supervised by the UN.

Among eucalyptus trees charred during the 1974 battle for Cyprus, Cpl. Benoit Champagne and Pte. Joel Langlois patrol a previously exclusive neighbourhood in Nicosia.

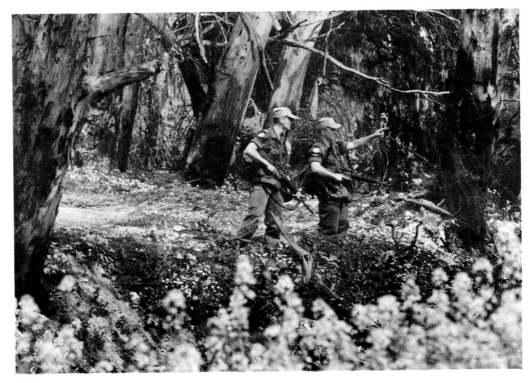

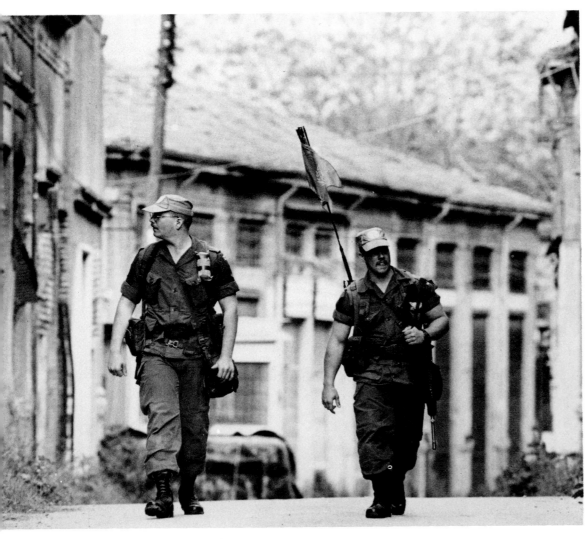

The largest and strongest contingent on the island, the Canadians are well equipped to handle day-to-day incidents in Nicosia. Here, peace-keepers at the Wolseley Barracks headquarters are inspected and sent out on their first patrol of the day.

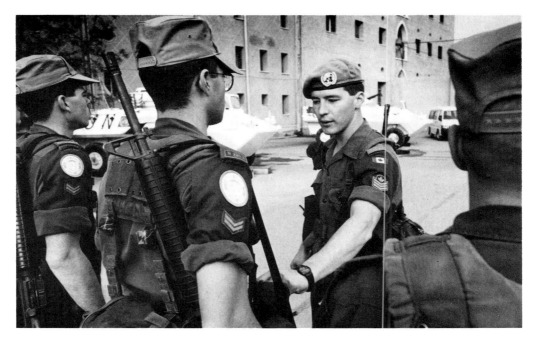

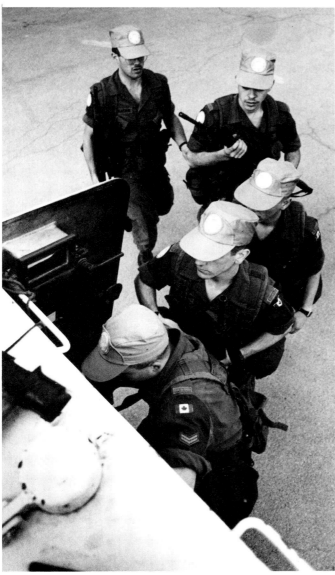

Apparent calm along the Nicosia "green line" can give way to violent confrontation with lightning speed. Canadian Grizzly armoured vehicles make patrolling this sector a safer and more effective task.

OPPOSITE:
Rolling out of Wolseley Barracks, a Canadian Grizzly takes to the streets, its crew alert for any signs of escalating tensions. "Military credibility is essential in the type of work we do," says Col. Robin Gagnon. "We carry a lot of firepower as a deterrent. Ideally we will achieve our mission without it."

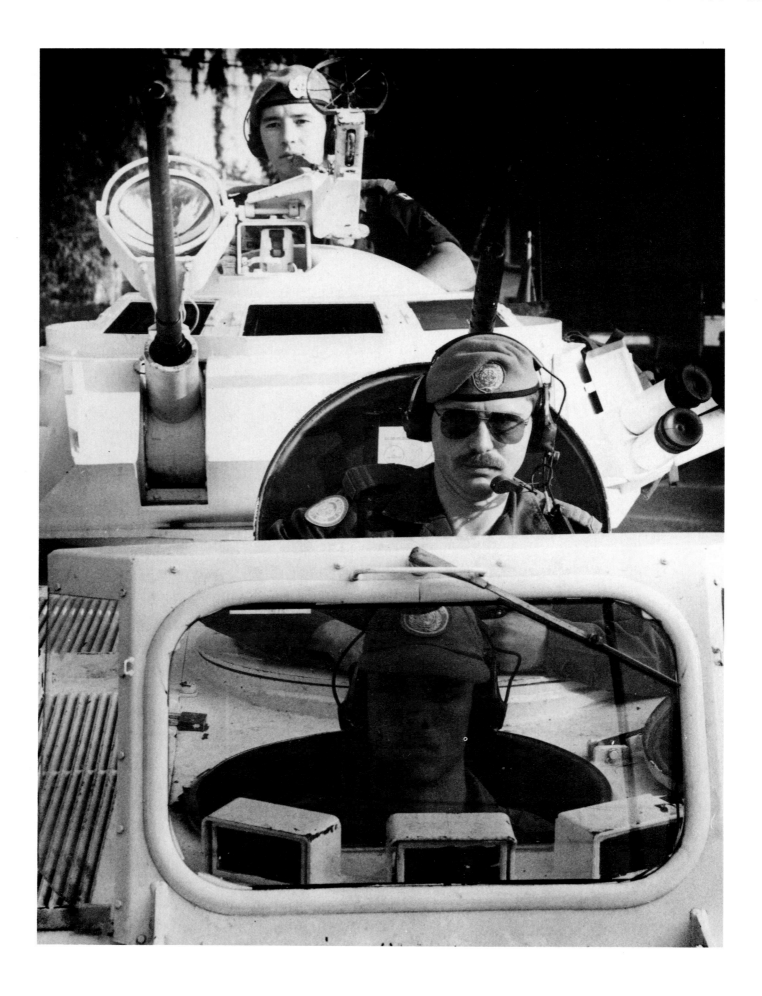

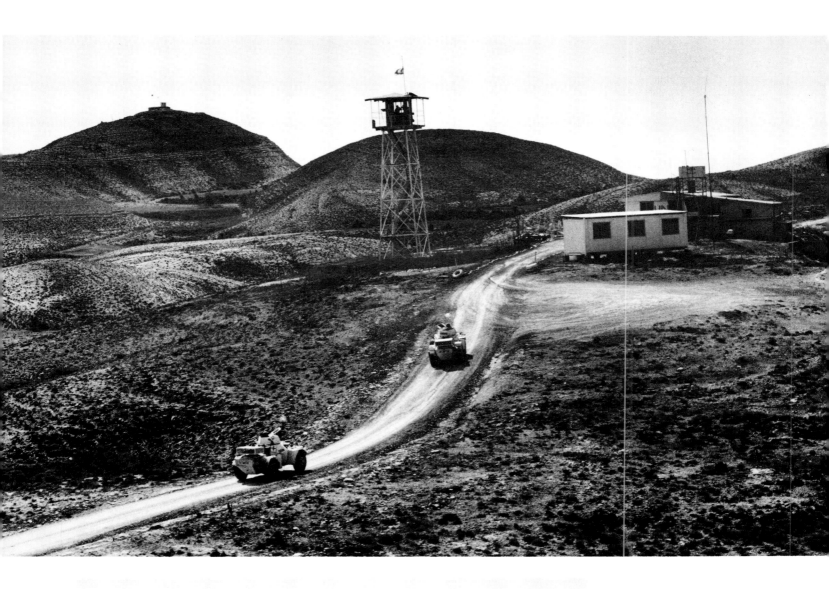

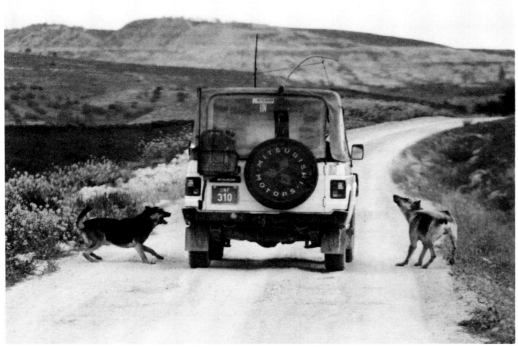

ABOVE:
Veteran performers on Cyprus, British Ferrets pass Observation Post 65 on a mobile patrol. The hilltop structure on the horizon is a Turkish lookout.

The UN jeep is a familiar sight on the winding roads of the divided island.

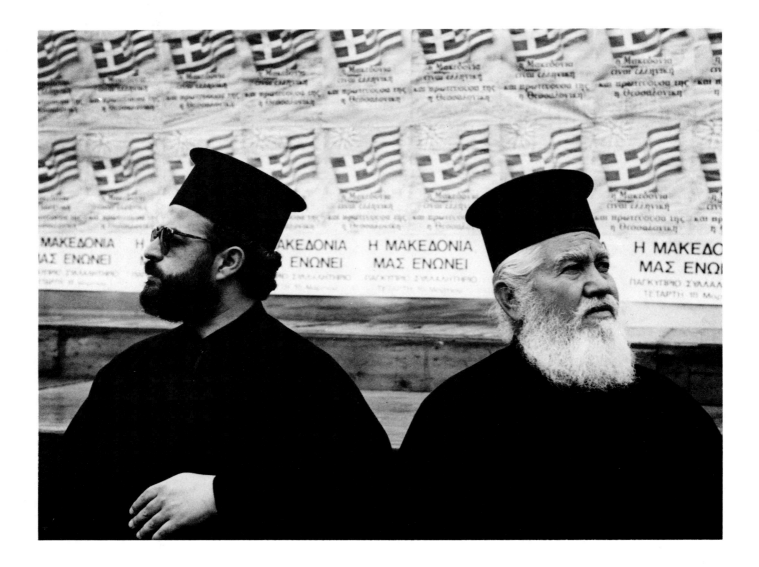

Powerful voices in the lives of Greek Cypriots, church and state are virtually inseparable. These Greek Orthodox priests are attending a political rally.

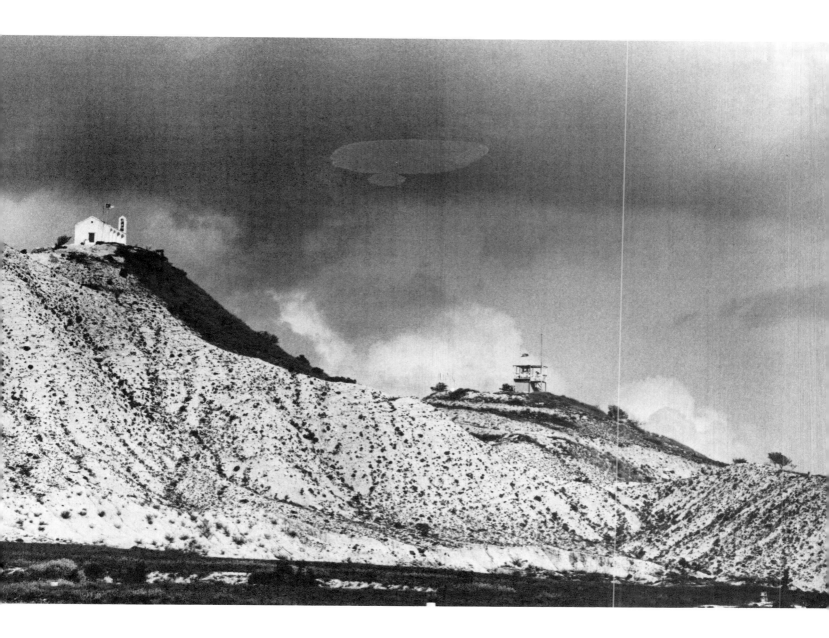

Holding the higher
ground, a Turkish Cypriot
church and stronghold
(*left*) overlooks a Canadian-
manned UN observation
post. Religion plays a less
political role in the lives of
Turkish Cypriot adherents
than it does among the
Greek Orthodox.

OPPOSITE:
Making up in *esprit de
corps* for the monotony
and solitude of Observa-
tion Post 65, the team
manning the 55-foot
tower avidly awaits
rotation back to Nicosia.
For most, the posting to
Cyprus is a six-month
tour. Some have done that
stint seven or eight times.

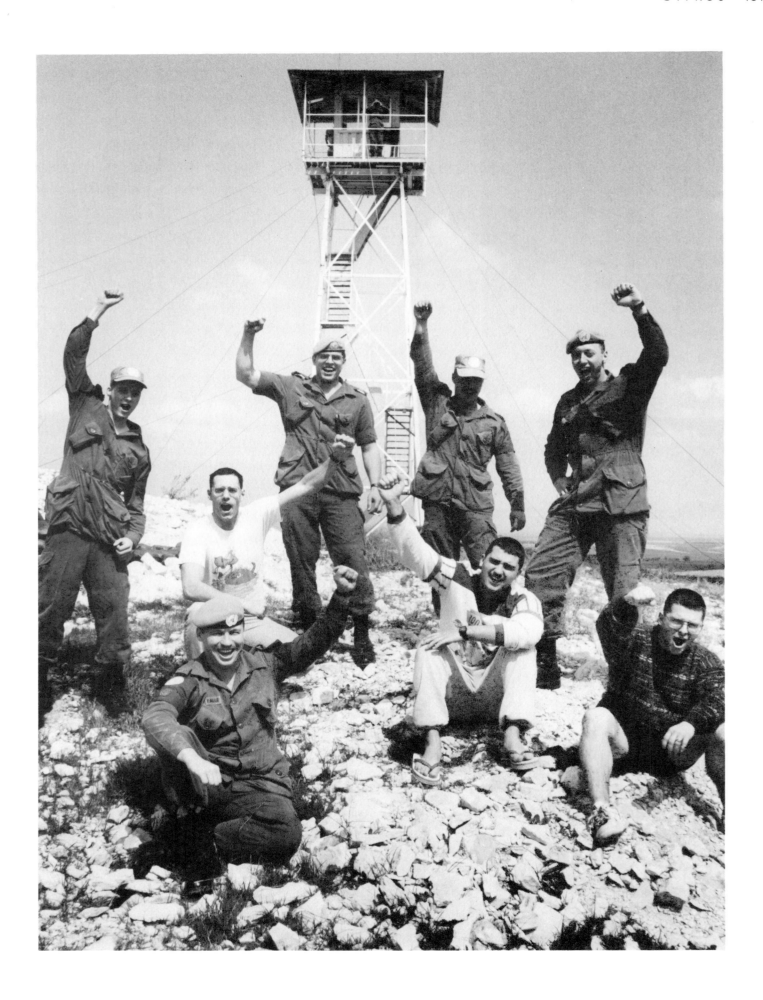

Touching down at isolated Observation Post 65, where Canadian observers scour the ceasefire line every hour of the day and night, a British UNFICYP helicopter brings news and supplies. The 141 observation posts provide a virtually unobstructed view along the *de facto* border.

Private Daniel Guevremont of Quebec City communicates with Wolseley Barracks while patrolling the buffer zone in Old Nicosia.

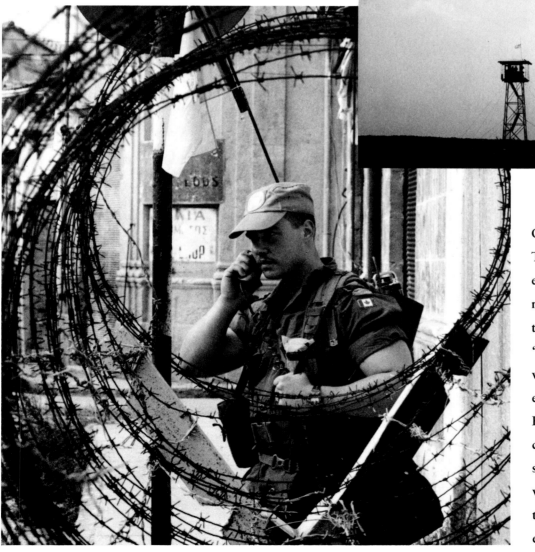

OPPOSITE: Though overshadowed by enduring hostility, a glimmer of hope may be on the horizon for Cyprus. "I was here in 1975. Shots were fired on the line every day," says Col. Robin Gagnon. "When I came back in 1979, those shots were heard only weekly. Today, none of the incidents involves an exchange of fire."

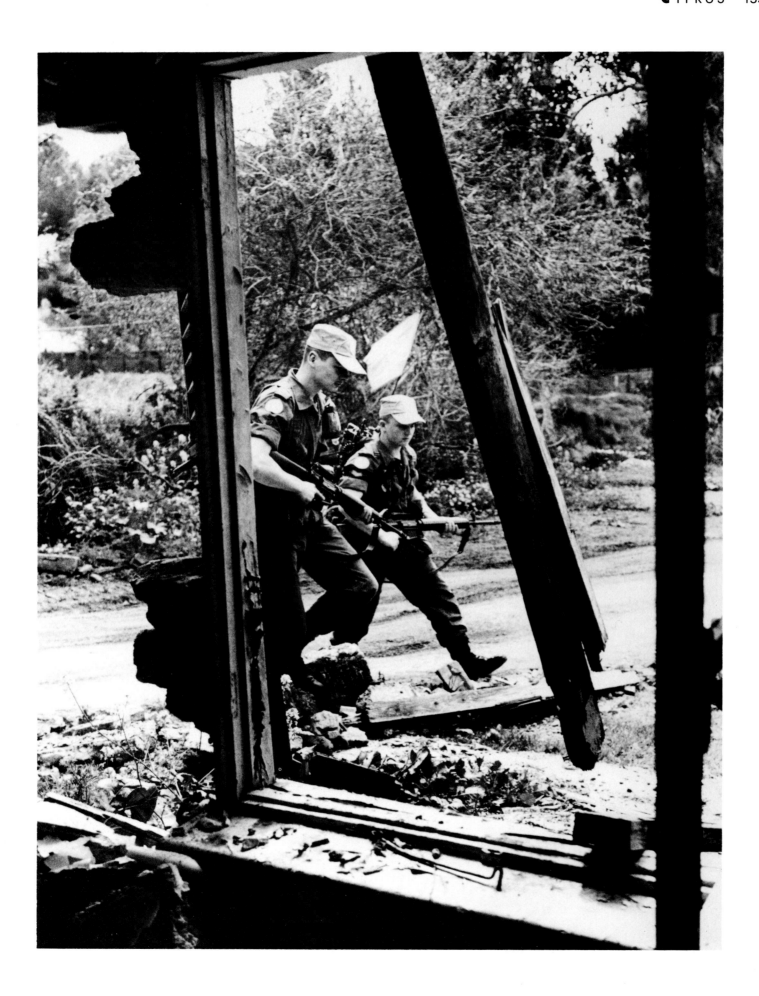

CENTRAL AMERICA

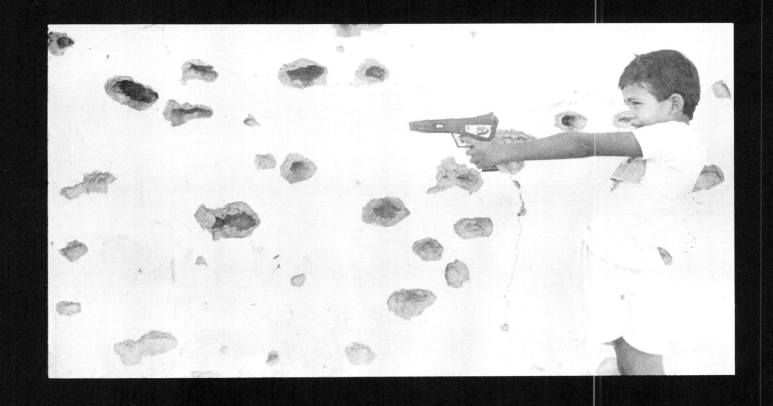

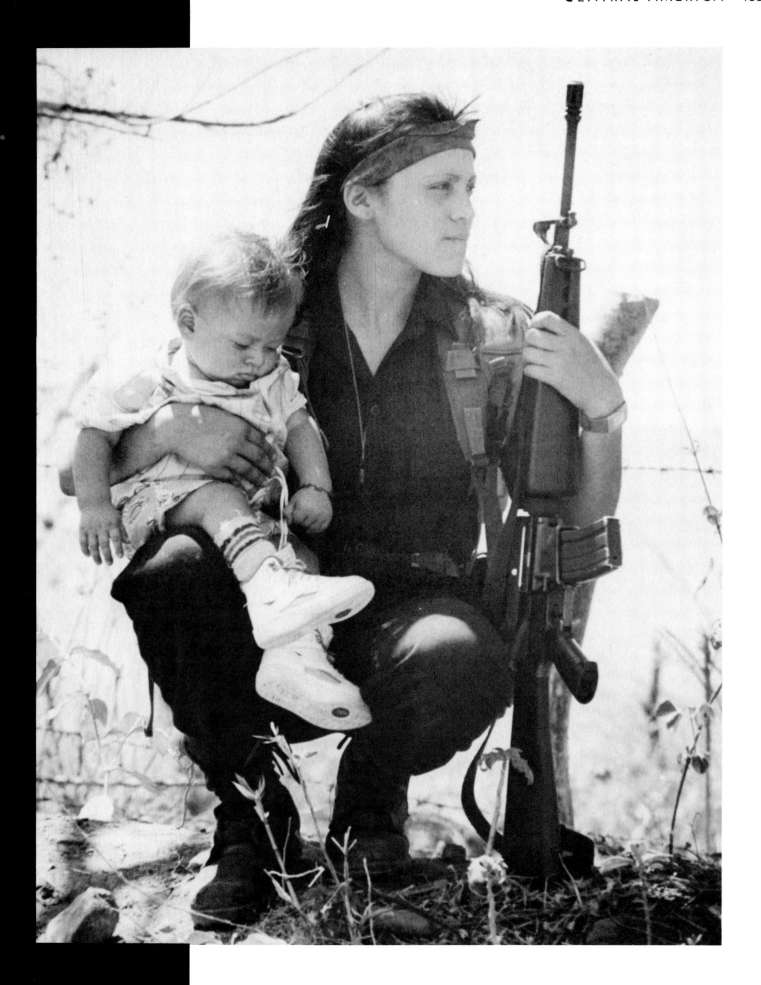

PAGE 134:

Child's play in El Salvador only a few years away from the real thing.

PREVIOUS PAGE:

Born into a struggle beyond their control, two young rebels are reunited during a gathering of guerrilla members in El Salvador's Guazapa hills. The 1992 ONUSAL ceasefire agreement, to which Canada contributed the second-largest UN observer delegation, was designed to bring the bloody 12-year civil war to an end.

UNTIL 1989 THE UN had played only the smallest of peacekeeping roles in the Western Hemisphere. Perhaps that was because the United States – brandishing the Monroe Doctrine, which was designed to keep Europe out of the Americas – considered this its own sphere. Certainly it was not because the area was a model of stability.

The coming to power of Fidel Castro in Cuba at the beginning of 1959, and his adoption of the Soviet model soon after, brought the Cold War to the hemisphere with a vengeance. The abortive Bay of Pigs invasion in 1961 and the Cuban missile crisis the next year made the risks clear to everyone, and the United States took steps to counter Cuban and Soviet expansionism in Latin America.

One sign of the proprietary American stance came in 1965, when a revolt in the Dominican Republic led the United States, bolstered by five other Latin American nations and a retroactive sanction from the Organization of American States, to send in troops to support the government. There was some disquiet in Ottawa over this intervention, and Canada provided one officer for the Mission of the Representative of the Secretary-General in the Dominican Republic, an observer mission that was in itself an expression of UN concern. The situation eventually stabilized, and the Americans and the UN mission were gone by 1966.

The Nicaraguan problem proved harder to resolve. The victory of Sandinista guerrillas over the Somoza dictatorship in 1979 brought another leftist government to power in Central America, and the United States and other nations in the region became convinced that the new Nicaraguan regime was the source of ideological and material support for other guerrilla movements, especially in El Salvador and Honduras. The Americans, for their part, provided arms and advice to the right-wing Contras, a guerrilla movement challenging the Sandinista regime, and to the governments of Nicaragua's neighbours.

Long efforts to start a peace process went nowhere. Finally, in March 1989,

The arid hills of central Honduras rise behind the Canadian peacekeepers stationed at Tegucigalpa. Of all the contingents involved in ONUCA – from Ireland, West Germany, Spain, Colombia, and Venezuela – the Canadian presence of 160 was the largest.

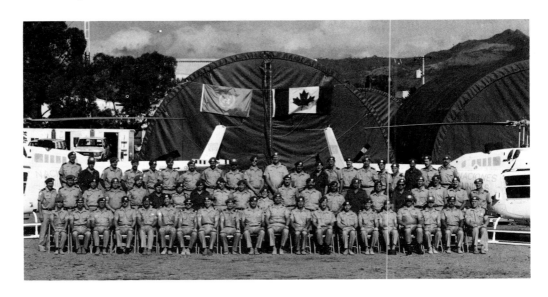

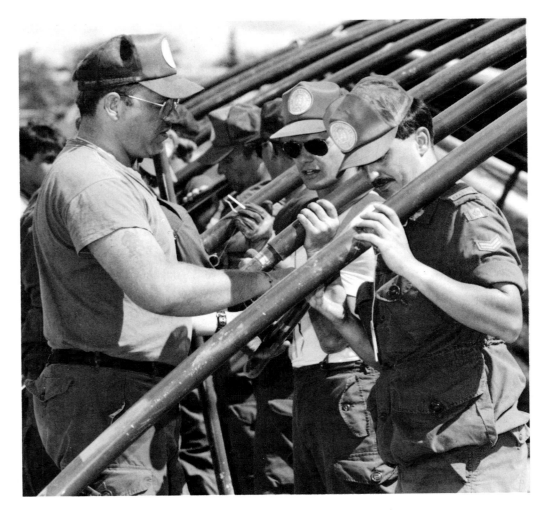

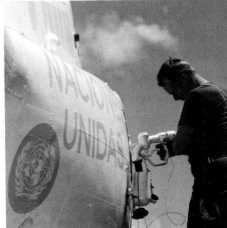

In a coordinated effort to keep the elements at bay, members of 89 Logistics Squadron with ONUCA erect a weather haven at Tegucigalpa Airport, Honduras.

A Canadian CH139 Jet Ranger helicopter is refueled at the Tegucigalpa base.

the presidents of Nicaragua and four other Central American nations called on the United Nations to establish a peacekeeping force. By mid-October, the Secretary-General had produced his plan for ONUCA, the Spanish acronym for the UN Observer Group in Central America. The plan called for a small mobile force of observers, with air and logistical support, to monitor Nicaragua's borders with Honduras, Costa Rica, Guatemala, and El Salvador. The participating states were to be West Germany, Spain, Colombia, Ireland, Venezuela, and Canada, with Ottawa providing forty officer observers and the air and ground crews necessary to keep eight helicopters flying. Despite fears that this situation might be as intractable as that in Cyprus, the Canadian government was willing to participate – but only on the condition that a ceasefire be in place from the outset. There was some hard experience behind that demand, and it was duly satisfied.

An advance party of Canadians left for Honduras on December 9; by late March 1990, the entire contingent was in place. By that time the situation had changed completely, as the Sandinistas had suffered defeat in Nicaraguan elections in February. A ceasefire agreement was signed by the Contras and Sandinistas on April 19. ONUCA supervised the demobilization of the Contras, destroyed

weapons, and provided a calming influence that allowed the Sandinistas to leave power in peace and with some grace. Very soon after, ONUCA began to wind up its operations, the first blue berets departing in June. The entire force shut down in January 1992 – yet another successful UN mission.

The end of the Cold War had obviously begun to alter matters in Central America. The disappearance of the Soviet Union meant that military aid to anti-government guerrillas in the region dried up. The defeat of the Sandinistas similarly removed a prop from the guerrilla movements. Fidel Castro's regime had been plunged into dire financial straits by the cessation of Soviet subsidies and oil shipments, and Cuba was now looking to its own difficulties first. Peace began to break out everywhere.

On January 16, 1992, the government of El Salvador and the Farabundo Martí National Liberation Front (FMNLF), which had waged a twelve-year guerrilla war against it, signed a ceasefire agreement. To superintend this agreement, the UN again sent in peacekeepers – including fifty-four Canadians, of whom twenty-four were posted in from the just-concluded ONUCA. The military peacekeepers were to monitor the concentration and progressive demobilization of the FMNLF, a process expected to stretch to October 1992, while a human-rights unit was to ensure that human rights were respected in police operations. Despite the usual complaints from each side about violations by the other, there seemed every reason for optimism.

A taste for haute cuisine, Puerto Cortés style, draws a master-corporal to the town's market area for lunch.

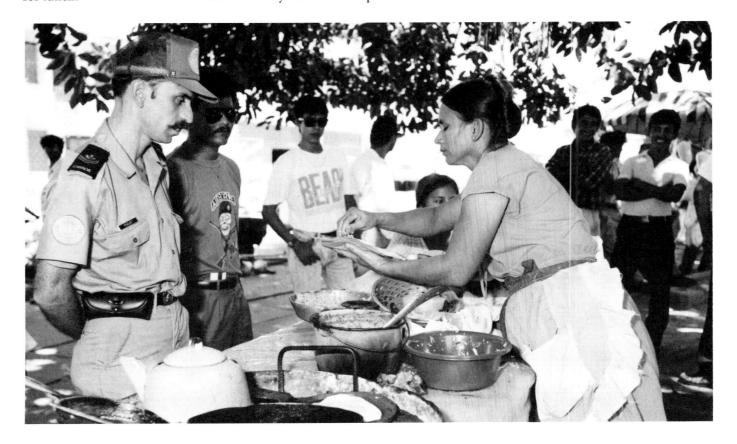

CALCULATED RISKS

BRIGADIER-GENERAL IAN DOUGLAS

Nicaragua

Our job in Central America was an observer mission. As opposed to ending a war with weapons, we were there to end it with our good offices alone, along with our military common sense and the respect of the forces we were demobilizing.

After we'd been there for some time, we decided it was up to us to take the initiative and visit Contra headquarters in the Yamales Valley. The Contras weren't keen on having us up there, but we felt strongly that it was part of our mandate, and they reluctantly agreed. We all knew the risks. As a precaution, we gave them pictures of our aircraft, hoping that if they knew what we looked like they wouldn't be so likely to shoot us down. It was no guarantee, though.

Our Canadian helicopters hadn't arrived by this point, so we had to rent from a company called Evergreen. Those guys really gave you an appreciation for the Canadian system. The first time I was up in one of their machines, I pulled the window open to get some air and the damn thing fell off! Flew out, disappeared! Another time, we were flying at about 700 metres over Lake Nicaragua and the bloody door came off. It certainly made one aware of the value of good maintenance.

Helicopters aside, flying into the Yamales Valley for the first time was one of my most exciting moments. I figured the most dangerous guy out there would be some kid with an AK-47 lying beside him, at the top of a hill, with nothing better to do than shoot at whatever flew overhead. So I had the pilot fly flat out, nap-of-the-earth, fast enough that we'd have come and gone before that kid had a chance to react.

As we turned into the valley, there was the Contra army spread out before us. Thousands and thousands of them. Company bivouacs, battalion bivouacs, family

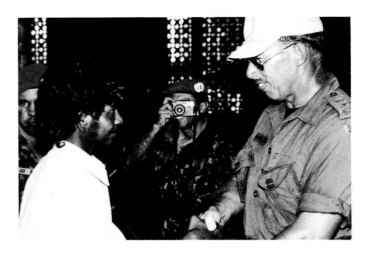

Brig.-Gen. Ian Douglas congratulates the first demobilized Contra of the Yatama Indians. "The feeling one got serving with ONUCA, bringing together people separated by war for so many years, is hard to describe. To see them talking again, acting like human beings. It was immensely gratifying."

bivouacs. It was lunch time, and they all seemed to be heading over to the kitchen area. No one fired on us, but we were right over their heads and you could see their surprise.

We flew up the valley three or four kilometres to the end of the encampment, crossed to the other side, and flew back down over a similar number of people. It was exciting as hell.

That was a calculated risk. It said, in effect: We're here and we have the duty to go wherever necessary. We had to make the UN presence visible, to get people to recognize the blue beret and the markings on our aircraft. It was a real operational breakthrough; it established our credentials.

Eventually, we demobilized an army of 23,000, helped repatriate them, helped reintroduce them to civilian roles. It is probably the most rewarding thing I've done in my life.

Brigadier-General Douglas was chief of staff for the UN Observer Group in Central America, in 1989–90.

ORPHANS IN THE VALLEY OF ANGELS

LIEUTENANT-COLONEL RICK FINDLEY

LIEUTENANT-COLONEL DAVE LOWDON

Honduras

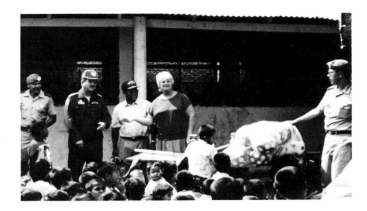

"The orphanage was badly in need of assistance," says Lt.-Col. Rick Findley (*second from left*). Here contingent members present a fund-raising cheque for $2,000.

LT.-COL. FINDLEY:

As part of the peacekeeping effort in Central America, Brigadier-General Ian Douglas suggested our squadron get involved in some sort of local community work. It's something of a tradition; we often contribute in this way during Canadian missions.

The contingent was headquartered in Tegucigalpa. With some research we found out about an orphanage in a village about thirty kilometres to the north. It wasn't sponsored by any of the churches or other charitable organizations, and it was badly in need of assistance. The village was called La Valle de Angeles – Valley of Angels.

Roughly 150 orphans lived in this place. It was spartan. What they needed more than anything was labour. We had a helicopter squadron, so we had technicians, electricians, mechanics, people with a lot of skills. We set to work fixing up the wiring, repairing appliances, and doing some plumbing.

Another problem was their water tower. It was in bad shape. We looked into different ways of fixing it up, but that job was left to the next rotation.

LT.-COL. LOWDON:

I was with the second rotation to Honduras. The guys in before us did a heck of a job, but they were busy getting established, and quite rightly tended to put administrative matters to the background. Our job as the second group was to get the operation on a sound administrative footing. We applied that same thinking to the orphanage.

We started by raising a fair amount of money. We held lotteries, collected donations, advertised throughout Canada. Fixing up the water tower was one of the major projects we inherited. We looked into it and found it would be more efficient to have it built locally than to do it ourselves. Instead, a lot of manpower was put into general repairs.

On the last Sunday, as the unit was being closed out, they assembled the orphans in the church and invited us to the service. The kids were all there, bright-eyed, singing their hearts out. It was hard not to be in tears, because these kids basically had nothing. It was a moving experience.

LT.-COL. FINDLEY:

The Hondurans are a very warm, very hospitable people. They are proud of their country, and were glad to have the turmoil finally ending. With peacekeeping, you don't always get to see the results of your actions. In Honduras, we did. Our work at the orphanage made the whole experience that much more meaningful. I often think our Directorate of Peacekeeping Operations would be better named "Peacekeeping and Humanitarian Assistance".

Lieutenant-colonels Findley and Lowdon were the commanding officers for the 89th Rotary Wing Aviation Unit of the 1990 UN Observer Group in Central America.

THE LAST DAY OF WAR

CAPTAIN GHYSLAIN BERGERON

Central America

As a maintenance test pilot in Honduras, I was one of the first Canadians flying the Twin Huey helicopter in Central America. The focus of the operation was assisting the UN in bringing about an end to the civil war.

After the last troops had laid down their weapons, a ceremony was held in San Pedro de Lóvago, a small town about 130 kilometres east of Managua. Most of the dignitaries and journalists were flown in. The Canadian Huey I was flying, as well as two others, carried mainly UN officials. The Nicaraguan president and press flew aboard three Nicaraguan Air Force Hip helicopters.

We arrived first and landed in a baseball field just north of the town. I knew the three Hips would need landing space, so we air-taxied close to the fenceline. When the Hips arrived, the first two landed on the ball diamond. The second wheeled up close to the first, probably to make room, before shutting down. Nonetheless, the third pilot elected to land outside the diamond, and it proved to be a very wise decision.

After the ceremony, most journalists got back into the Hips for the return trip to Managua. The Hip is a huge helicopter, almost as long as a city bus. When the second helicopter lifted into an unsteady hover, it crept forward and its main rotor clipped the first helicopter's tail rotor. The pilot pulled back on the controls, his tail rotor contacted the ground, and when I last saw it flying, the helicopter was banked 90 degrees on its left side with the main rotor blades digging and beating into the grass.

In an effort to limit further damage, the pilot sitting in the first helicopter lifted off, but he couldn't control the huge aircraft without its tail rotor. It too crashed seconds after takeoff, in a field on a gently sloping hill only a hundred metres or so from the first crash site.

The first Hip was right in front of us, no more than 50 metres away. The engines were still running even though it was lying on its side like a beached whale.

When helicopters get imbalanced, parts start flying. They beat themselves to death. That's what happened next. Parts of the aircraft started whistling all over the place. Then it caught fire.

I grabbed one of our extinguishers and ran over. It was really starting to smoke by now and people were running away in every direction, like the spokes of a wheel.

The turbines were starting to disintegrate and I knew that a metal fire would be very hard to put out. I got up close and stuck the extinguisher straight down into the tailpipe. I emptied the extinguisher and the fire almost stopped. But then a big leak of oil and fuel gushed down and there was no way of getting the fire out.

The Hips have a big fuel reservoir inside. It's like five 45-gallon drums, just like a big milk tank on a farm. That's their gas tank. There were a couple of explosions as the reservoirs started to go, but you never knew when the big one was going to occur. Whenever I'd hear an explosion it would send a bit of adrenalin into the system and I'd dash away for a minute. I was thinking, when this thing blows, it's probably going to take our helicopter with it.

I ran around in the smoke to the other side of the aircraft. I tried to open the clamshell doors but I couldn't reach the snaps. I ran back around and saw that one of the pilots was trapped inside. He was getting barbecued in there, really getting smoked.

One of his crew members was outside too, and we both got in and grabbed him. He was semi-conscious, gashed on the forehead pretty bad. We got him about fifteen metres away and then other people started giving us a hand. We were sort of dragging him and running. We had to get the hell out of there.

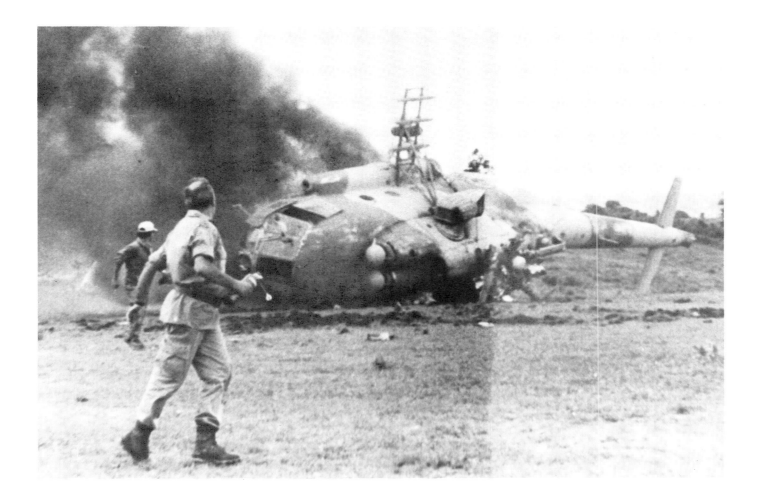

The Hip has a nose-mounted gun, and either that one was loaded or there was ammunition in the cockpit. No more than two minutes after we got the pilot out, the bullets started going off. Then there were massive explosions, probably boxes of ammunition going up.

We were worried about stray bullets and there was more panic, but our helicopter wasn't hit. We loaded up the most seriously injured, and medivaced them to Managua. There was a lot of blood but I think everybody lived.

Next morning, it was all over the papers. Lots of pictures. Don't forget, all those journalists were right there when it happened. What does a journalist do once his life has been saved? He starts taking pictures. There were shots of everything, pictures of me going in to get the pilot, even shots of the fireball when the thing exploded.

"Whenever I'd hear an explosion . . . I'd dash away for a minute," says **Capt. Bergeron** about his **1990 rescue effort** of a **Sandinista pilot** trapped in a blazing helicopter. "One of the pilots was trying to grab me and I could hear him shouting that the whole thing was going to explode."

When I got back home and my mother found out what had happened, she was a little upset. Well, very upset. But that blew over. By the time I got the medal, she was quite happy.

It was just something I had to do. That was their last day of war. The next morning was to be their first official day of peace.

A member of the 1990 UN Observer Group in Central America, Captain Bergeron was awarded the Medal of Bravery.

PEACE ON THE HORIZON

LIEUTENANT-COMMANDER GRAHAM DAY

El Salvador

It was like a porcupine that has walked into a fishing net. The peace process in El Salvador was a very, very complex intertwine – lots and lots of spikes sticking into many many sections of the net. We were there to see that all those spikes – small guerrilla bands and small army detachments – were disentangled and moved farther apart.

The mission was a brand-new concept for the UN, really a visionary concept. It was very exciting to be part of it. As military observers, we were one leg of a triad. We worked closely with UN police forces and human-rights observers. In that respect, it was a new wave in peacekeeping.

I've been around the world several times with the navy. I served eight years in submarines. I was what we called a "deep cold warrior". We fought the Cold War and it was clear who our enemy was.

That war is over. America and Russia are no longer facing off against each other. The world has changed. A lot of old pressures are gone, and new pressures are building. The real agenda for the next century will probably not be ideological, but more fundamental – human rights, environmental issues.

I volunteered for the job in Central America to see if this new internationalism really had anything to it. In El Salvador I came to realize that we are not just warriors for our own country now, we are becoming warriors on behalf of more basic values, for the entire world.

What made me feel really good about our work in El Salvador was the people. I'd be shopping for groceries after work and Salvadorans would see my uniform and come up. They'd shake my hand, hug me, kiss me. They'd say, "Thank you. We want peace and we are pleased the UN has come. We know you will help us." It would make a lump come to my throat and my eyes start to moisten. I can tell you, in Canada nobody has ever come up and hugged me and kissed me in a supermarket except my wife.

The sad part was the children in uniform. I was observing government troops securing a landing zone one day. Two of the soldiers were young teenage females. They were very professional, very thorough. When they finished, they reported back to their officer. Then they took off their rifles and packs and started doing each other's hair. I thought of my boy Alexander, the same age. Those Salvadoran kids have had a large chunk cut out of their lives. The civil war robbed them of youth they will never know.

We made a difference. The Salvadoran people have a lot of passion, a lot of gusto. They paint with bright colours. They will come through. My profound feeling is that peace is on the horizon for El Salvador.

Lieutenant-Commander Day was a military observer with the UN mission to El Salvador in 1992.

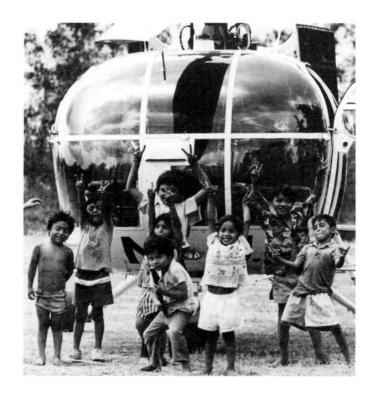

Excited by the arrival of a UN helicopter, Salvadoran children congregate to meet the peacekeepers they know it carries.

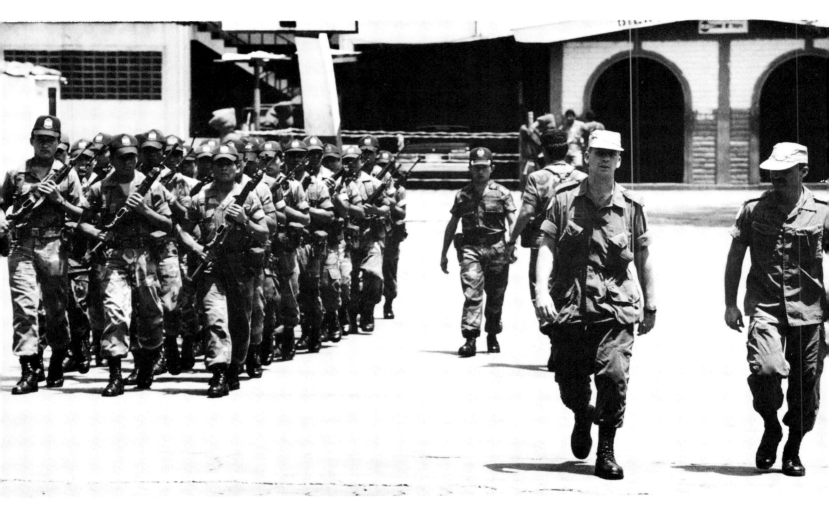

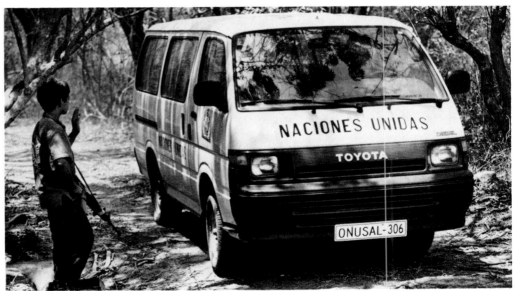

ABOVE:

Flanked by a Salvadoran
army unit at San Vicente,
Capt. Bruno Di Ilio (*far
right*) and Capt. Pierre
Noel (*next*) help monitor
demobilization of the
force's counter-insurgency
battalions, and the reduc-
tion in size of the government's armed forces to
roughly half their original
strength.

A child guerrilla guards
the entrance to FMLN
Camp Murillo.

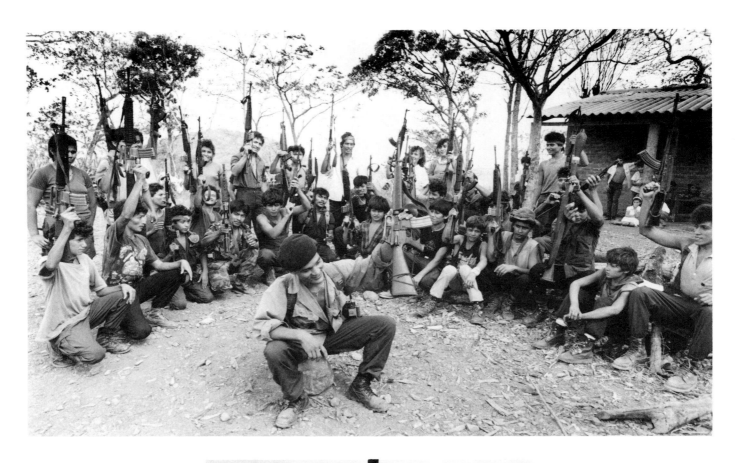

ABOVE:

Saluting UN efforts at a verified and sustained peace, the peasant army of the FMLN in Santa Clara look forward to the day when they can relinquish their weapons and return to their fields.

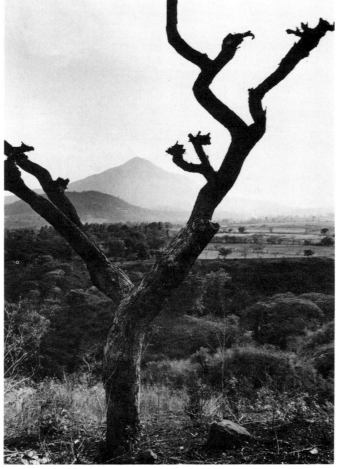

The view near San Vicente and Santa Clara is deceptively peaceful. The foothills which separate guerrilla forces and government troops remain heavily mined.

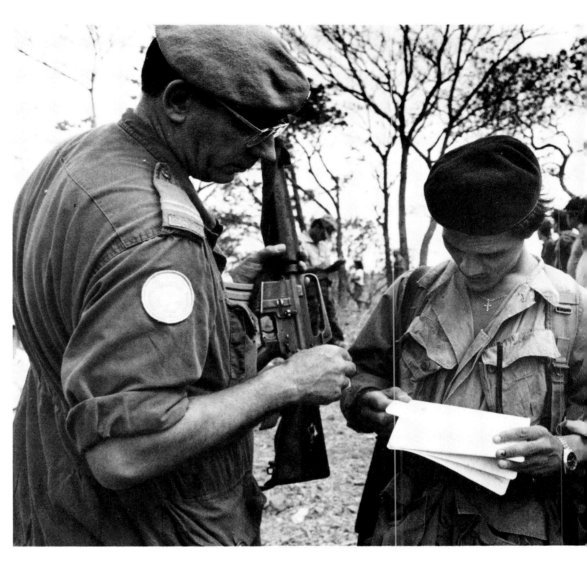

Arms, explosives, communications devices – the Murillo encampment of the FMLN boasts a menacing arsenal. Each piece must be itemized and later accounted for when the guerrilla bands demobilize and hand over their weapons.

DATOS DEL ARMAMENTOS, EXPLOSIVOS, MUNICIONES Y COMUNICACIONES DEL FMLN
VT MURILLO

1. ARMAMENTOS.

(A) PISTOLAS	(B) FUSILES (i) M 16 - 16 (ii) AK 47 - 09 (iii) M 14 - 01 (*) CARABINA M1 - 05	(C) SUBAMETRALL- -ADORAS	(D) MORTEROS	(E) RPG 2	(F) RPG 7	(G) M 72-A2
H) CAÑON 57	(I) CAÑON 75	(J) CAÑON 90	(K) SAM 16	(L) GR.M.INDUST	(M) GR.M.CASERAS 50	(N) M-79
O) M-26	(P) MINAS	(B) AMETRALLADORAS (R)	(S)	(T)	(U)

2. EXPLOSIVOS Y MUNICIONES.

A) MECHA LENTA	(B) TNT	(C) NITRATO	(D) INICIADORES	(E) GR 57	(F) G.R 75	(G) GR 90
) GR. MORT	(I) GR M 26	(J) GR M 79	(K) 7.62 mm 348	(L) 5-56 mm 1599	(M) 38 mm 302	(N)

. COMUNICACIONES.

) HANDY TALKIES	(B) PRC-77	(C) ICOM 01	(D) SPILBURY	(E)	(F)	(G)

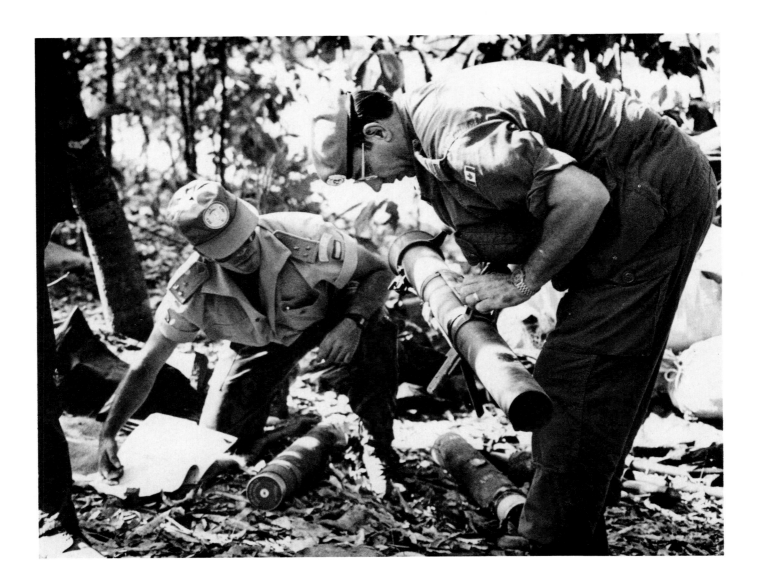

OPPOSITE AND ABOVE:
Capt. Newman and the
verification team inven-
tory the Santa Clara
unit's heavy weaponry.
Although scattered
factions resisted the UN
mission – firing a rocket-
propelled grenade into
UN headquarters shortly
after it was established –
most Salvadorans sup-
ported the accord and
welcomed the UN
presence.

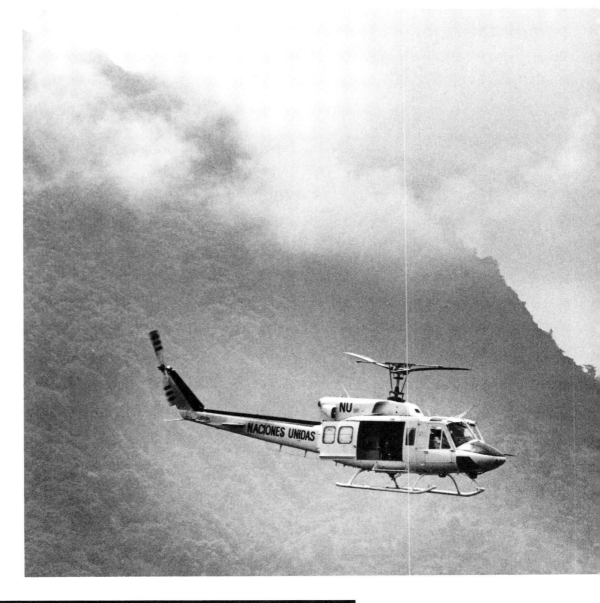

BELOW:

On the approach to El Roblillo, Lt.-Col. Hank Morris (*left*), ONUSAL's chief operations officer, directs the helicopter's Ecuadorean pilot. "One thing I've always enjoyed about flying," says Morris, "is that it focuses all your concentration. You're right out there on the edge. Everything seems to become quite clear, even though you may be very much afraid."

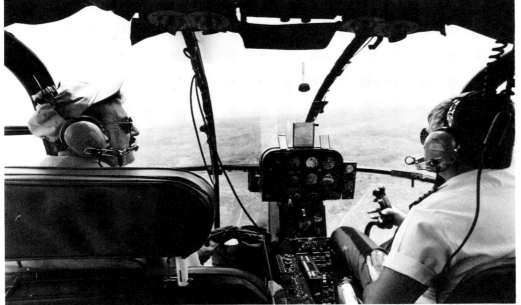

ABOVE:

Skirting the volcanic peak of Guazapa on El Salvador's rugged border country, an ONUSAL helicopter nears El Roblillo, mountain stronghold of insurgent FMLN forces.

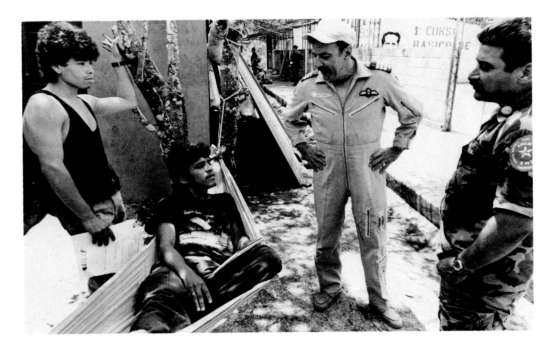

"'Where is your gun?' – It's the first thing they ask me," says Lt.-Col. Morris about meeting young FMLN fighters. When they learn I'm out here with nothing but my good will and a little blue badge, it makes a big impression." These ex-guerrillas are studying for positions with the newly established Salvadoran police force.

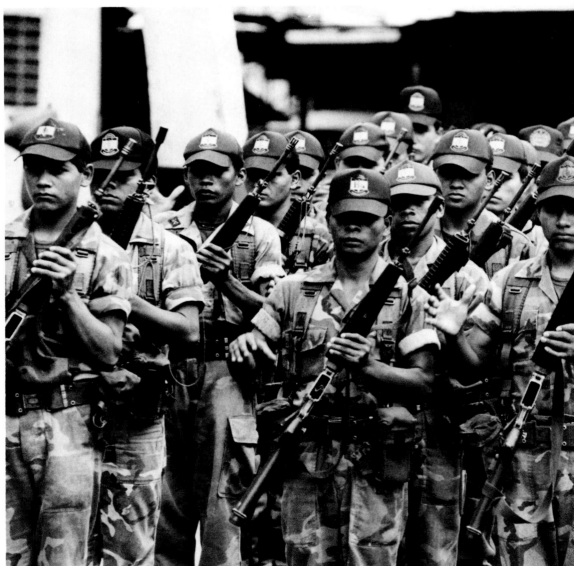

Marching to an uncertain future, Salvadoran government troops include soldiers in their early teens – many "recruited" from the streets and public meeting places.

Under a billowing FMLN banner in El Salvador's coastal jungle, a cook in the Murillo guerrilla camp prepares what may be one of their last meals together as the UN monitors the disbanding of their organization.

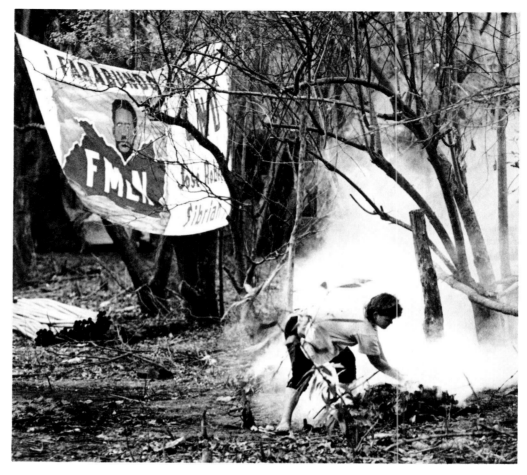

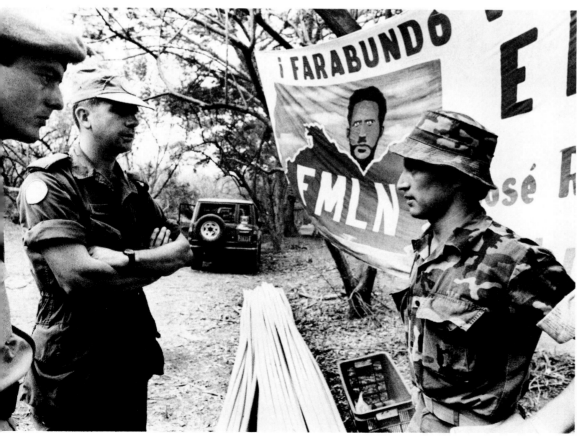

At the Murillo encampment, Capt. Pierre Noel and a Spanish colleague meet camp leader Maj. Sergio Da Silva. All told, 7,000 to 8,000 FMLN troops and more than 30,000 government troops will demobilize. "I don't think anyone won this war," says Lt.-Cmdr. Graham Day. "It was not winnable by either side. That's why they're sticking to the ceasefire. They know the alternative."

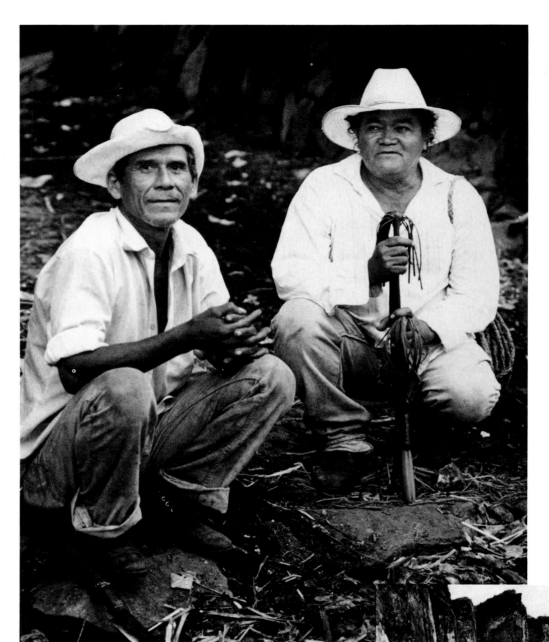

For the *campesinos* the hostilities have been a nightmare. "The war has stopped. It's given El Salvador a chance," concludes Lt. Col. Hank Morris. "We've done our part. Now it's up to them."

Destroyed in retaliation for guerrilla attacks, a bombed-out church lies exposed in the FMLN village of Aguacayo. "As every new day passes without armed confrontation," says Lt.-Cmdr. Graham Day, "El Salvador gets closer to a lasting peace.

THE PRICE OF
PEACE

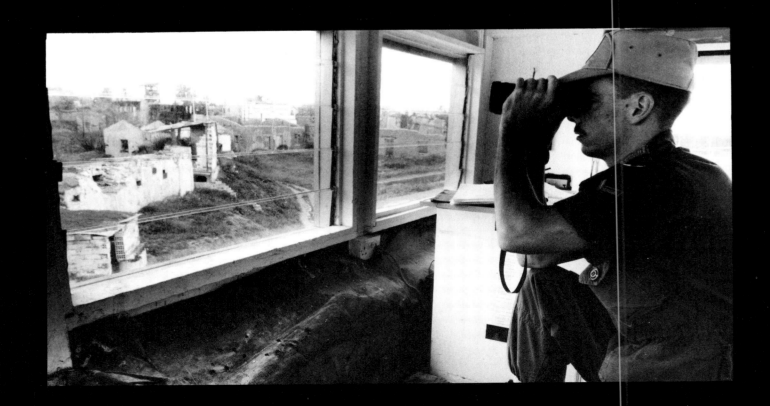

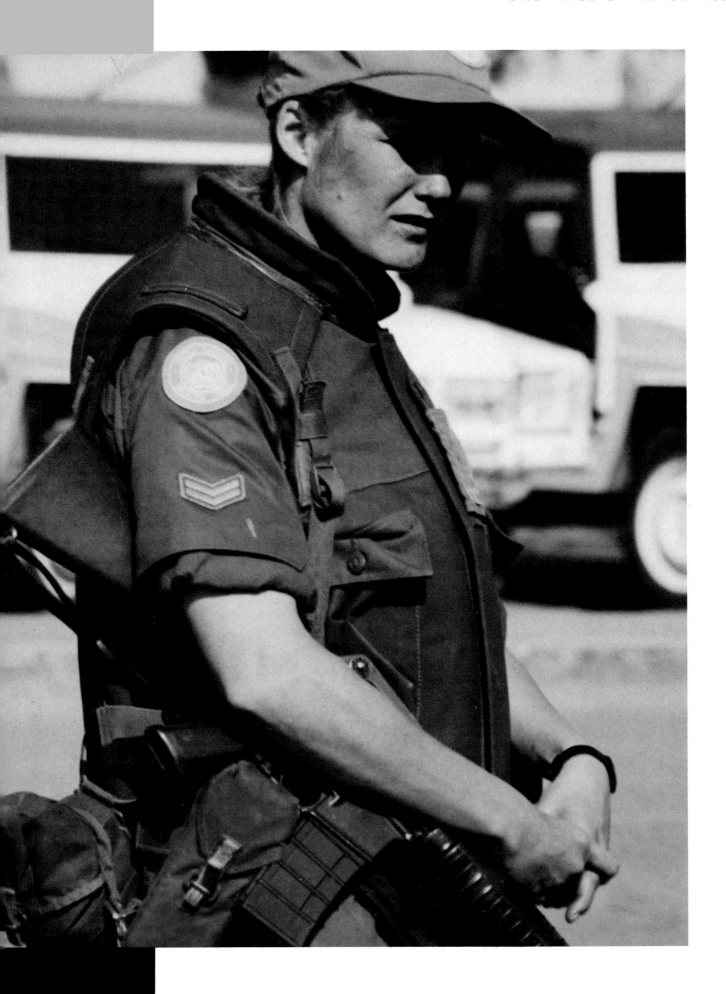

PAGE 152:

Keeping watch on Turkish and Greek Cypriot positions only 30 metres apart, Pte. Michel Fortin mans Observation Post 45, at Omorphita. Each post is equipped with a bunker from which observers can maintain communications with headquarters in the event of serious hostilities.

PREVIOUS PAGE:

Canadian troops serving under the auspices of the UN made it possible to deliver desperately-needed relief to the beleaguered civilian population of Sarajevo and Daruvar in the summer of 1992.

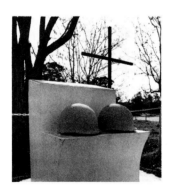

Lost in the service of peace. This simple monument in Nicosia's Wolseley Barracks is dedicated to the 27 Canadians who have died while serving with UNFICYP.

AFTER ALMOST FORTY-FIVE years of peacekeeping, what lessons have been learned? More than 85,000 Canadian servicemen and servicewomen have served under the United Nations flag in operations around the globe, and as this book is published some 2,500 are on duty in Central America, the Middle East, Africa, Cyprus, Yugoslavia, and Cambodia. Eighty-three Canadians have died on UN duty, striving to keep the peace.

That peacekeeping is useful seems beyond doubt. Without the presence of the blue berets, the Namibian elections would not have been held in relative peace, the Turkish and Greek Cypriots would be at each other's throats, and the Congo might have continued in chaos. Peacekeeping works – once the combatants are tired of fighting and genuinely want a solution – and the awarding of the Nobel Peace Prize to United Nations peacekeepers in 1988 was ample testimony to that. Canadian Armed Forces personnel believe, and not without reason, that they have done more than their share to earn that prize.

Unfortunately, many members of the UN have not wanted to pay the costs of the organization's operations, and the United States and the former Soviet Union are the major defaulters. UN rules allow contributors to peacekeeping operations to receive payment for their military costs. But while Canada spends $12 million to $15 million a year, above pay and allowances, to keep its troops in Cyprus, Ottawa accepts only some $2 million in compensation from the UN, swallowing the rest as a contribution to world peace. Now, with massive new UN operations under way in Yugoslavia and Cambodia, the financial situation is becoming desperate.

Despite shortages of specialists, our armed forces have been very efficient in every UN role they have been called upon to fill. They have been observers or participants in supervisory roles; they have monitored elections; they have filled military roles. That they have shown such flexibility and skill is a tribute to their training – and, though many Canadians fail to realize it, this training has been for war. Well-trained servicemen and servicewomen can easily assume a peacekeeping or "policing" role, for discipline and responsiveness have been inculcated into them. But a police officer, on the other hand, cannot play a wartime role without a prolonged period of training. In a world as unstable as that of the 1990s, when crises spring up abroad or at home, only well-trained and well-equipped members of the armed forces can be ready to handle the necessary variety of peacekeeping roles.

Why is Canada called upon so often? It is not because we occupy some high moral ground. It has not been our self-image as a quasi-neutral democracy that has made us so desirable for peacekeeping. Rather, it was Canada's position as a committed member of the Western alliance that saw us serve on two separate International Control Commissions in Vietnam. It was our membership in NATO

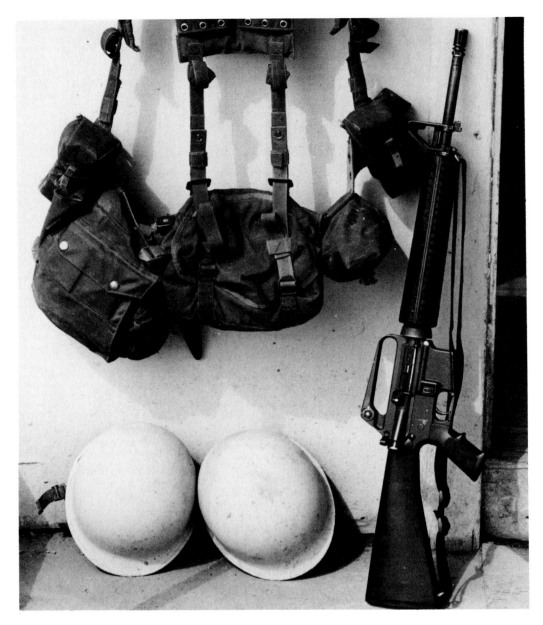

Although UN peace-keepers only use force as a last resort, the fact that they are well armed helps to prevent problems. "You're right in the middle. Every day there are shouting matches," says Maj. Gilles Linteau about Cyprus. "Last week a Turkish recruit took his weapon and aimed it at one of my soldiers." Fortunately the encounter was quickly defused.

and the Commonwealth that led us to Cyprus. It was the skills and training of the Canadian Armed Forces that made us the providers of signallers to the Congo and Iran–Iraq. And it was the fact that Canada had always planned its military forces for overseas service that gave us the air transport and logistical capabilities that made us essential in UNEF, UNDOF, ONUCA, and the MFO. Neutrality had nothing to do with it, in other words.

The end of the Cold War and the collapse of the Soviet Union have removed the central threat to the West's existence. It will be a tragedy if the lesson Canadians draw from this is that they can dismantle the armed forces that have served them so well. That mistake was made in 1919, and to a lesser extent in 1946. It must not be made yet again, if peacekeeping – an essential element of our hope for a peaceful future – is to continue to receive Canada's full support.

PRISONER EXCHANGE

CAPTAIN MICHAEL ROULEAU

Yugoslavia

My posting to Yugoslavia always calls to mind the devastation, the vast destruction all across the front. Unlike a lot of other peacekeeping operations, this was no standoff. You'd go to a town one day, and when you went back a week later it would be destroyed. The civil war was going strong. Ceasefires would hold for a couple of hours, then be broken.

Our main job was observation, monitoring anything from breaches of ceasefire, to troops being evacuated back into their home territory. I was on escort-convoy duty one day, and as our convoy penetrated no man's land I was flagged down by a Croatian colonel. He was frantic. He said, "Things have gone to shit here. You've got to help us. We don't have any EC [European Community] people here, and we need somebody to monitor a prisoner-of-war trade."

I walked up to the vehicle where the Croatian prisoners were held. As I passed it I just glanced in the side window, and this gaunt animal face stared back out. It was all I could do not to jump away in fright. He didn't look much like a man at all.

We signed the papers and then both sides had to verify the identities of the prisoners. As their names were called the Croatians climbed out of the van. They all had their chins touching their chests, obviously something they had been schooled to do during their time in captivity. With their heads down, and each head touching the head of the prisoner in front, they walked forward like a big caterpillar. They wouldn't look up. Most were badly beaten; two were carried out on stretchers.

There was a real air of tension. Everybody had Kalishnikovs and hand grenades hanging off them. Eventually we persuaded them to go back to their positions. We were unarmed, but the blue and white EC colours carried a lot of weight.

When you're in a situation like that, you tend to think about your life and your priorities. Imagine: these people had been held for months. There I was, a Canadian officer from the other side of the world, helping them finally get back to their own sides. After you've done something like that, you can't help but get a big lump in your throat and say: We did something good today.

Captain Rouleau participated with the eleven-member Canadian contingent of the European Community observer group posted to Yugoslavia in late 1991.

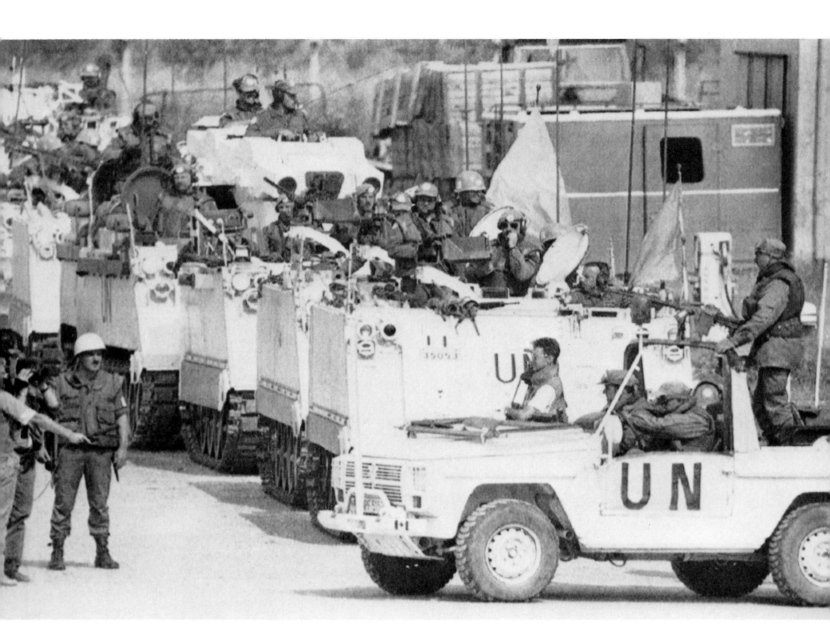

The first 100 vehicles
carrying Canadian troops
arrive in Sarajevo airport
as part of the UN relief
mission to Bosnia in
July 1992.

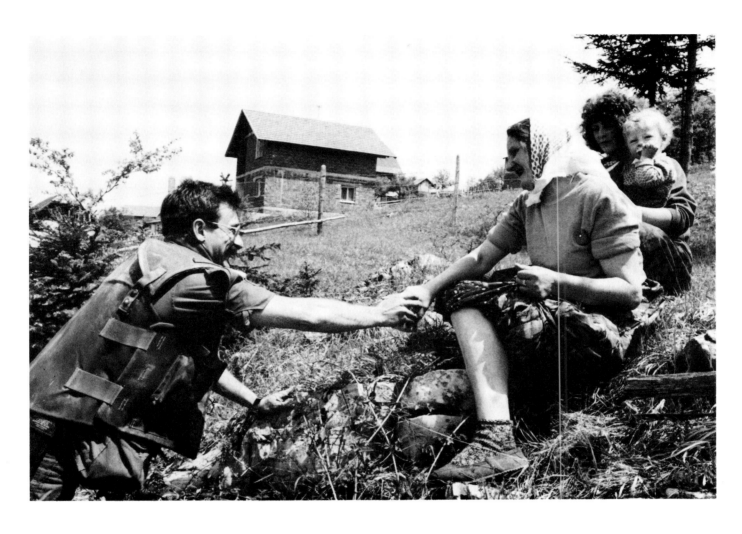

Master Seaman Monty
Penney shares food from
his rations with a civilian
family near Sarajevo.

OPPOSITE:
Maj. Alex Fieglar passes
out candies as he disem-
barks at the helipad near
ONUSAL headquarters in
downtown San Salvador.
As a more substantial
move, the Canadian
government is providing
funds for rebuilding the
houses of returning
peasants who fled as
refugees to Honduras
during the worst years
of the war.

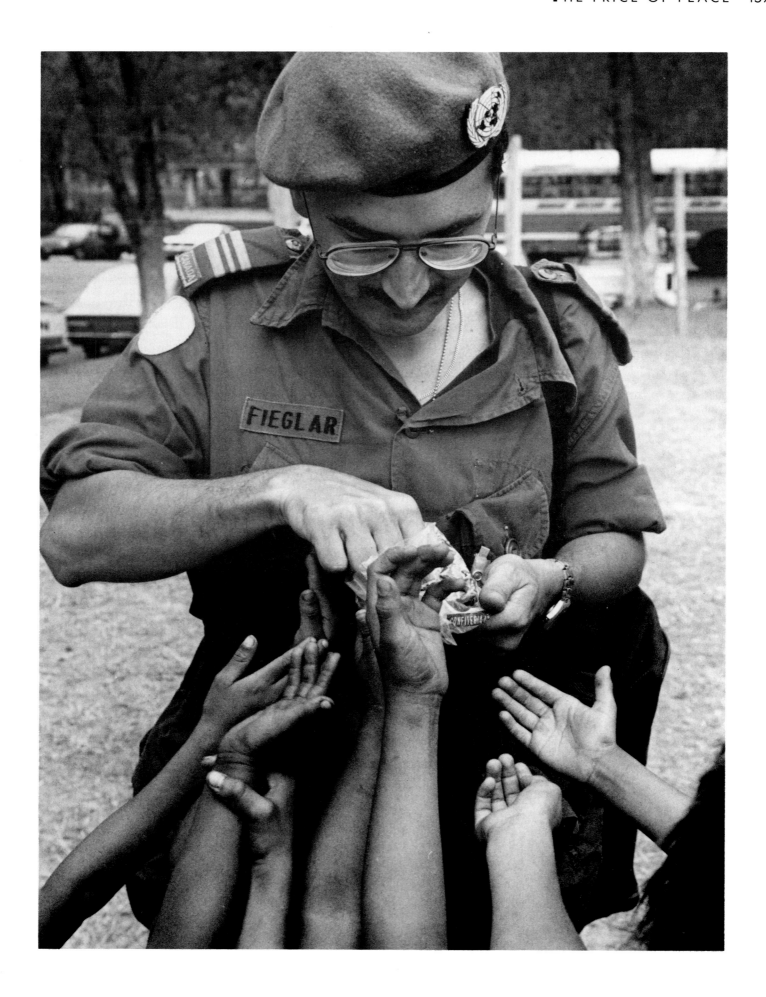

PHOTO CREDITS

Photographs in the mosaic on pages 2-3 all appear elsewhere in the book, and are credited accordingly. All photographs are by Boris Spremo unless otherwise indicated.

The following abbreviations have been used:
DND   Department of National Defence, Rockcliffe Base
NAC   National Archives of Canada

Page 5: Canapress;
15: Luis Romero;
18: Canapress-AP;
19: DND (ISC88-1210-14);
20: Emile Ashawi;
21 top: NAC (C18969); *bottom:* NAC (PA113009);
22 top: DND (ME108); *bottom:* DND (PL107482);
23: DND (ME733);
24 top: John Muller; *bottom:* DND (ISC84-315, Vic Johnson);
25 top: DND (CF67-370-18); *bottom:* DND (IS75-3);
26 top: DND (PL146475); *bottom:* DND (PL107581);
27 top: DND (RE75-1494); *bottom:* DND (ISC78-315);
28: Brad Olmstead;
29: DND (PL146468);
30 top: Brad Olmstead; *bottom:* DND (PL146466);
31 top: Gilbert Côté; *bottom:* Vern McKeen;
33: Gordon Bennett; *inset:* Geordie Elms;
34: Geordie Elms;
35: DND (ISC84-274, Vic Johnson);
36: Brad Olmstead;
37: DND (ISC88-1211-32);
38: Bob Scott;
39: Gordon Ramsay;
40: Gordon Ramsay;
82: Canapress-AP (G5803)
83: DND (VNC73-434);
84: DND (PMR74-834);
85: DND (PMR74-829);
86 top: DND (IOC89-13-27); *bottom:* United Nations;
87: NAC (PA151200);
88 top: DND (VN73-273); *bottom:* DND (VN73-065);
89 top: DND (VN73-063); *bottom:* DND (PCN73-245);
90: DND (VN73-276);
91: DND (VN73-134);
93: DND (TN72-57);
94: Geordie Elms;
95: Deborah Wolfe;
96: Deborah Wolfe;
98: DND (UNC64-009-15);
99: DND (UNC63-096-8);
100: DND (PC2411);
101: DND (PMR82-775);
103 top: DND (PC2396); *bottom:* DND (UNC63-009-6);
104 top: André Seguin; *bottom:* André Seguin
105: André Seguin
106: DND;
111: DND (PCN74-903);
112 top: DND (CYP71-196A); *bottom:* DND (CYP74-154);
113 left: DND (IXC88-341, John Smith); *right:* DND (CYP66-303-3);
114: DND (IXC88-349, John Smith);
115: DND (CYP74-123-36);
134: Luis Romero;
135: Luis Galdamez;
136: DND (IXC90-095);
137 left: DND (IXC90-032); *right:* Rick Findley;
138: DND (IXC90-012);
139: I.C. Douglas;
140: I.C. Douglas;
142: Henry Morris;
153: DND (ISC92-5079);
157: Canapress;
158: DND.

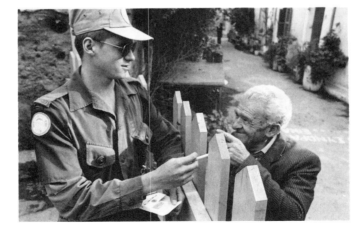

Pte. Martin Pare offers a cigarette and a friendly ear to a Greek Cypriot whose community borders the buffer zone.